TRACING THE CONSEQUENCES OF CHILD POVERTY

Evidence from the Young Lives study in Ethiopia, India, Peru and Vietnam

Jo Boyden, Andrew Dawes, Paul Dornan
and Colin Tredoux

First published in Great Britain in 2019 by

Policy Press
University of Bristol
1-9 Old Park Hill
Bristol
BS2 8BB
UK
t: +44 (0)117 954 5940
pp-info@bristol.ac.uk
www.policypress.co.uk

North America office:
Policy Press
c/o The University of Chicago Press
1427 East 60th Street
Chicago, IL 60637, USA
t: +1 773 702 7700
f: +1 773-702-9756
sales@press.uchicago.edu
www.press.uchicago.edu

British Library Cataloguing in Publication Data
A catalogue record for this book is available from the British Library

Library of Congress Cataloging-in-Publication Data
A catalog record for this book has been requested

978-1-4473-4831-3 paperback
978-1-4473-4836-8 ePdf
978-1-4473-4837-5 ePub
978-1-4473-4838-2 Mobi

Cover design by Hayes Design
Photo credits: The images throughout our publications are of children living in circumstances and communities similar to the children within our study sample.
© Young Lives/Nguyen Quang Thai; Trinh Van Dang.
Printed and bound in Great Britain by CMP, Poole
Policy Press uses environmentally responsible print partners

Contents

List of figures and tables

Figures

Tables

Notes on authors

Jo Boyden is Professor of International Development/Director of Young Lives, Oxford Department of International Development. She is an authority on child development and children's rights and has worked on research and policy with children, particularly child labour, education, children in conflict, as well as publishing on childhood resilience in the context of adversity, poverty, and socio-cultural development.

Andrew Dawes is Associate Professor Emeritus in Psychology at the University of Cape Town and a Research Associate with Young Lives. His expertise includes the development indicators for measuring children's rights and wellbeing, prevention of child maltreatment and violence to young children, and evaluations of early childhood development programmes in African settings. He has extensive experience in translating research to policy.

Dr Paul Dornan was Senior Policy Officer at Young Lives in the Oxford Department of International Development. He is a social policy analyst with expertise in social policy and child poverty and was responsible for leading policy activity within Young Lives.

Colin Tredoux is Professor of Psychology, University of Cape Town, South Africa, and Chaire d'Attractivité, CLLE, Université de Toulouse, CNRS, UT2J, France. His interests in Social Psychology include contact theory, and the micro-ecology of contact and segregation. He has published widely in a range of journals, including *American Psychologist*, *South African Journal of Psychology* and *Psychological Science*.

Acknowledgements

Young Lives has been a collaborative partnership between 12,000 study children, their families and their classmates, research institutes, universities and non-governmental organisations (NGOs) in four study countries, and a team based at the University of Oxford, together with researchers at University College London and other universities in the UK and USA. We are hugely grateful to the children and families who have participated in the study. Without their generosity, patience and willingness to talk to field workers regularly over a period of 15 years, often about sensitive subjects, the Young Lives study and its rich dataset would not exist. Special thanks are also owed to our collaborators, and to our research, communications and policy teams, data managers, field supervisors, and all other Young Lives staff for their contributions to so many aspects of the study, from the rigorous research design, high-quality data and publications, to the vital administrative support and robust engagement with policy and practice. Sharon Huttly merits special mention for her conscientious and steadfast stewardship of Young Lives during an earlier phase of the study, which created an essential foundation for the later research.

This book has benefited from the contributions of many people – although any errors are of our own making. In particular, we wish to thank Deborah Walnicki, who played an invaluable research assistance role by analysing qualitative data and sifting through interview transcripts for appropriate quotes, drafting selected texts, undertaking literature searches and compiling and checking references. Deborah displayed considerable flexibility, patience and good humour, despite the multiple demands placed on her. The book synthesises analyses produced by numerous study colleagues and reflects their careful and important work. It also draws on new work by Kristine Briones, Gina Crivello, Joaquin Fuenzalida Concha and Ginny Morrow. Marta Favara and Patricia Espinoza-Revollo have generously given time throughout to respond to data questions.

Additionally, we are grateful for the insight, guidance and support of a distinguished advisory group, Frances Stewart, Richard Morgan, Martin Evans, Dominic Richardson and Catherine Porter. We are indebted to Santiago Cueto, Angela Little, Richard Morgan, Alula Pankhurst, Anne Peterson, Martin Woodhead and members of the Young Lives International Advisory Board, for reviewing various elements of the work and providing meticulous and constructive feedback. We have benefited from opportunities to present earlier drafts of this work to the Department for International Development (DFID), the Global Coalition to End Child Poverty and Save the Children and appreciated thoughts and comments.

Young Lives was initiated and core funded from 2001 to 2018 by UK aid from DFID. The vision, resources, advice and direction provided by many DFID staff over the years have been fundamental to the study's longevity and success. Further research and policy engagement has also been funded by the Bernard van Leer Foundation, the Bill & Melinda Gates Foundation, the Children's Investment Fund Foundation, the Dr Mortimer and Theresa Sackler Foundation, Echidna Giving, the Economic and Social Research Council (ESRC), Grand Challenges Canada, the Inter-American Development Bank, the International Development Research Centre, Irish Aid, the Medical Research Council, the National Institutes of Health, Netherlands Ministry of Foreign Affairs, the Norwegian Embassy in Vietnam, the Oak Foundation, the Old Dart Foundation, Open Society Foundations, Oxfam GB, the Oxford Martin School, Plan International, Save the Children UK, UNESCO, UNICEF, the William and Flora Hewlett Foundation and The World Bank. We are extremely grateful for the support given by these organisations, their financial contribution building on the core DFID-funded research to enable deeper analysis of specific topics and broadening Young Lives' sphere of influence.

Core-funded by

ONE

Introduction: From surviving to thriving?

'Nothing is impossible for me.'

These are the words of Hadush,[1] a 13-year-old boy from a farming family in rural Tigray, in northern Ethiopia. The Young Lives study has been interviewing Hadush and his family, together with thousands of other children and families in Ethiopia, India (in what are now the states of Andhra Pradesh and Telangana), Peru and Vietnam, since 2002. Hadush's mother died when he was young, and his family is poor. Although Hadush has received little schooling, he is ambitious for the future; he hopes to get a good job so that he can lift himself and his family out of poverty. Children and families across the study share this ambition. Yet, sadly, many of them are unlikely to realise their dreams. As a unique longitudinal inquiry into the lives of children in the first two decades of the 21st century, Young Lives shows many of the reasons why. The study began in 2001, and was initiated by the UK government's Department for International Development to inform policies and programmes to improve the prospects of children like Hadush. Young Lives has been collecting detailed information on a wide range of topics – including health, nutrition, education, time use and psychosocial wellbeing – from 12,000 boys and girls living in diverse sites across the four study countries, as well as from schools attended by some of the children. After more than 15 years of research, the evidence now spans the first two decades of life, from ages 1 to 22 years. This book summarises the key findings generated by Young Lives research and discusses implications for child-focused policy and programmes across low- and middle-income countries (LMICs). It is our hope that these findings can support efforts by countries to meet the challenges set out in the Sustainable Development Goals (SDGs; UNGA, 2015).

A study of the children of the millennium

Young Lives was set up during a period of optimism for global development associated with the Millennium Declaration (UN,

2000), with the aim of informing the Millennium Development Goals (MDGs) to reduce poverty. At the time, data on child poverty in LMICs were scarce and inconsistent. It was clear, however, that this was a very significant problem. The United Nations International Children's Emergency Fund (UNICEF) estimated in 2000 that half a billion children, 40% of those in LMICs, were living on less than a dollar a day (UNICEF, 2000). Indeed, children are consistently over-represented among the poorest people in all countries and are also particularly vulnerable to the consequences of poverty. Even taking account of the young populations in low-income countries, the headcount poverty rate for children is higher than that for adults (UNICEF and The World Bank, 2016; OPHI, 2018).

The scale of child poverty is one of many concerns. There is also growing recognition of its multidimensionality, since material deprivation is only one of the many disadvantages typically experienced by poor children. This means that reducing poverty involves more than simply raising income, important though this is. Children growing up in poverty are often deprived of quality education, water, sanitation and other services, and suffer poor nutrition, and poor physical and mental health. To reflect this complexity, the United Nations Development Programme (UNDP) employs the Human Development Index, a country-level composite measure made up of indicators of life expectancy, years of schooling and gross national income (GNI) per person. Although it is not disaggregated by age, the index is intended to capture multiple dimensions of human development and not only economic growth. Figure 1.1 summarises changes in the Human Development Index in the four Young Lives countries over the period of the study, comparing these with wider regional trends.

There were important national and regional improvements in human development during this period, due in part to rising GNI, particularly in Ethiopia, which has the lowest human development ranking of the four. The post-2000 period involved rapid economic growth and policy development across many regions of the world. Conditions for children improved significantly on measures of both extreme monetary and multidimensional poverty. Recent figures drawing on the rebased extreme monetary poverty indicator (US$1.90 per person per day) suggest that on this measure child poverty fell from 737 million children in 2002 to 409 million by 2012 (Watkins and Quattri, 2016). The extreme monetary measure does not capture all of what matters for children, since child mortality has also fallen, and school enrolment rates have risen in virtually all countries. Improvements in water and sanitation access have been marked, as have innovation and

Figure 1.1: Human development, 2000 and 2014

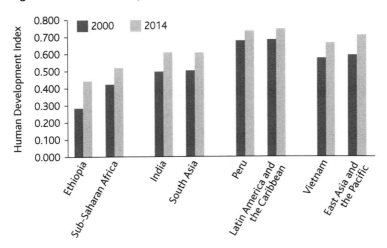

expansion in social protection. However, the survival and basic needs of children in conflict-affected countries remain a major concern. The slowest progress was made in sub-Saharan Africa, which – taking into consideration demographic trends – now accounts for the highest proportion of the poorest young people globally.

Policy challenges ahead

As in many other LMICs, the governments of the four Young Lives countries have over the past two decades stressed the importance of economic growth in national planning and expanded the scope of social policy. This expansion is evident in new social protection schemes and increased infrastructure. There has also been progress in aspects of child protection (for example, reduction of hazardous child work), health, education and preschool policy. The SDGs provide a platform for further gains for children in the study countries and elsewhere. The SDGs are broader in scope than the MDGs and include eradicating poverty and hunger, promoting good health and wellbeing, and achieving clean water and sanitation, along with a number of other goals and targets of direct relevance to child health and development. Even so, and despite impressive advances for children in recent decades, three major policy challenges remain, and these apply in both Young Lives countries and across much of the Global South.

First, while the MDGs have been associated with remarkable progress in child survival and development, the poorest in society have not always benefited or have benefited less than other groups. In many or most countries across the globe disparities in income and wealth have become entrenched. There is rising concern about the extent of economic inequality and its impact on wellbeing and development (Piketty, 2014; Atkinson, 2016; The World Bank, 2016a). Economic growth improves average living standards, but it cannot be relied on to narrow gaps within countries and will widen them if growth is not equitably shared. This is the context for the call to 'leave no one behind' expressed in the SDGs, which set an ambitious agenda for human development to achieve by 2030. The SDGs represent an advance on the MDGs in their consideration of inequality and the requirement that data be disaggregated to draw attention to the situation of the most disadvantaged populations. As children are more deeply affected by poverty than other age groups, progress for the poorest children is essential to make this vision a reality. This book highlights the factors perpetuating inequality between different groups of children and discusses a role for policy in ameliorating the conditions confronted by the most disadvantaged.

Second, despite progress made in reduced child deaths during the MDG period, this has not yielded similar gains in other aspects of children's wellbeing. For example, many children remain in poor health and many are also undernourished, leading to growth stunting and associated loss of developmental potential. Many thousands are exposed to violence in their homes, schools and communities. Furthermore, there is growing recognition of a learning crisis, in which raised enrolment and attendance has yet to be translated into quality learning and new work opportunities for the young. Improving learning and reducing the learning gaps between rich and poor within and across nations involves reform of education systems. But the success of education policy is also dependent on circumstances well beyond the control of schools, such as whether children have sufficient nutrition to ensure they can concentrate in class, or whether caregivers have the time and skills to support children with their homework. Improving learning outcomes therefore implies increasing the effectiveness of multi-sectoral action, including greater responsiveness of services to children's home circumstances, as well as better alignment and coordination across sectors. This book outlines how children can benefit from these links and opportunities for enhancing policy measures.

The third challenge has to do with sustaining investments from early childhood through the first two decades of life. There is consensus within developmental science that very early periods of life are vitally important for all that follows later. Policy-makers are heeding that message, including through expanded early childhood programmes. Nevertheless, prioritisation and resourcing lags behind the science. Developmental science, including findings presented in this book, is now increasingly highlighting how later stages also matter. Indeed, recent work has called for a focus on the first 8,000 days of life (Bundy et al, 2018), from conception through to early adulthood. Child development requires not only a firm foundation but sustained investment through middle childhood and adolescence, in age-appropriate ways. As such, adolescence (and early adolescence in particular), is increasingly understood as a second critical window for intervention. Programming across the life course needs to start early, but should also be sustained through childhood, both to avoid early gains being lost and to remediate early harms. This book examines both the timing of investments and what is important for different children at different stages of childhood and adolescence in order to contribute to policy-making that adopts a life course approach to planning for children.

Young Lives study countries

The comparative design is one of the most powerful features of the Young Lives research. The four study countries reflect a broad range of political-economic and human development circumstances. The sample is also large and diverse, spread across the study countries. Where common findings are found across the four countries, their external validity is evident. This means that the findings are very likely to apply to other countries and contexts. The World Bank classifies Peru as an upper middle-income country. Both India and Vietnam 'graduated' from low- to middle-income status over the study period. Ethiopia remains a low-income country, although it, too, has seen rising gross national income. But, as this book shows, the relationship between economic development and wider human development is not simple. For example, Vietnam consistently surpasses India in human development indicators, despite a similar GNI per capita, and sometimes outstrips Peru, despite a much smaller GNI. While the size of the economy is significant for human development, history and policy choices also matter.

The following provides some key information about the four study countries.

Ethiopia is one of the world's poorest countries. In addition to a civil war and rule by the repressive Derg military regime from 1974 to 1987,

Ethiopia is highly vulnerable to drought. Over recent years the federal government has twice declared a state of emergency. Nevertheless, in recent decades the country has had one of the fastest-growing economies in Africa, with an average growth in gross domestic product (GDP) of 10.9% per year between 2004 and 2014 (The World Bank, 2016a). Infrastructure and services have expanded, and new industrial zones have been created. Extreme monetary poverty halved from 55% in 1996 to 33% by 2011, with rural and agricultural households making most progress (The World Bank, 2016a). However, like most other countries in this period, income inequality has increased, meaning that the gains were unequally experienced (Concha, 2017). Ethiopia's estimated urban population grew rapidly from 12 million to 19 million between 2005 and 2015 (UN Habitat, 2016). Urban job opportunities for those without post-secondary qualifications are limited (The World Bank, 2016a). A large proportion of households remain dependent on rain-fed agriculture. The country is regionally prominent and the capital, Addis Ababa, hosts the headquarters of both the African Union and United Nations Economic Commission for Africa.

The Ethiopian government's pro-growth focus is shown by the 'Growth and Transformation' plans that have been used to steer development objectives. National policies have been key in driving increased access to services – particularly education – and to social protection. School enrolment has been rising consistently. A programme involving the deployment of health extension workers was launched in 2003 to improve basic health conditions. Nevertheless, basic health problems persist, including high rates of child stunting. The history of drought and famine motivated the creation of the Productive Safety Net Programme, a large-scale social protection programme implemented in 2005 and directed at food-insecure parts of the country. Most recently (since 2010), an ambitious plan has been devised to add a year of preschool prior to formal school entrance at 7 years of age. With the rapid scaling up of public programmes, the government is faced with considerable challenges of resourcing, a lack of capacity for implementing changes, and problems of ensuring quality of delivery. Additionally, Ethiopia has a high fertility rate and half its population is aged less than 18 years (UNICEF, 2017). The country vividly represents some of the challenges facing low-income countries in sub-Saharan Africa at present, and likely in the future too, given expectations of continued growth in the size of the youth population. The large youth population represents a potential 'demographic dividend', but to reap returns from this trend requires meeting the hopes for better jobs and decent livelihoods. If better options do not exist for young people, not only will individual hopes be dashed but future national development undermined.

In **India**, Young Lives was originally established in what was then the state of Andhra Pradesh, in the south east of the country on the coast of the Indian Ocean. Now divided into two states, Andhra Pradesh and Telangana (termed United Andhra Pradesh – also UAP – in this book), the combined population was 85 million at the time of the 2011 census.[2] Compared with other Indian states, United Andhra Pradesh is neither the poorest nor the most economically advanced. Many of the trends affecting United Andhra Pradesh reflect wider patterns across India. Between 2005 and 2015, India's urban population increased from 330 million to 420 million, a rise from 29% to 33% of the total population (UN Habitat, 2016). Between 1994 and 2012, extreme poverty fell from 45% to 22% and The World Bank argues that on current trends India will reduce extreme poverty to below 3% by 2026 (The World Bank, 2018a). Nevertheless, many people remain poor and structural inequalities based on gender, ethnicity and caste prevent significant sections of the population from accessing economic opportunities. There are also considerable differences in circumstances between urban and rural areas, such as different livelihood prospects, and different degrees of access to sanitation and other basic services.

As with the other study countries, there has been substantial policy innovation over the period since 2000. Important examples include the large-scale Mahatma Gandhi National Rural Employment Guarantee scheme (2006), the 2009 Right to Education Act and the 2013 Right to Food Act. A new strategic planning process, which has replaced previous Five-year Plans, places economic transformation and growth centre stage (Government of India, 2017). However, not all communities have benefited equally from strong growth, poverty reduction and social policies. Many households and children remain excluded from basic services and service quality remains a concern. For education, there has also been a rapid increase in parents and children opting to use private over government schools. Of the Young Lives countries, India is where discrimination against girls and women is the most prominent and most entrenched. Early marriage is common (Roest, 2016). India is among the lowest ranked group of countries on the UNDP Gender Development Index (UNDP, 2016). Although they receive considerable policy attention, Scheduled Tribes[3] and Scheduled Castes also face consistent discrimination and children from these groups are very disadvantaged and have less access to services than other children.

Peru is the most economically advanced of the Young Lives countries and recently its economy has been one of the fastest-growing in Latin America. By 2000, Peru was already a predominantly urban society, with 71% of the population living in urban areas. Extreme poverty fell from 16% to 4% between 2004 and 2015, with faster income growth for the poorest households resulting in a decrease in inequality (The World Bank, 2017). The World Bank also notes that income from labour increased over this period, and that this contributed to lower poverty and lower income inequality.

Nevertheless, Peru's performance on human development indicators is mixed. The country has a history of conflict, with the Shining Path insurgent movement active, mainly in rural areas, until quite recently. Despite its comparative wealth, Peru faced a significant problem of child under-nutrition at the turn of the millennium. Stark differences remain evident between the predominantly Spanish-speaking coastal region and cities, such as the capital Lima, and the largely rural Andean and Amazonian regions, where indigenous groups and languages are more common. Rural areas face high levels of poverty and insecurity, and even though service access has improved in these areas over the period of the study, rural populations have less access to basic services and those services that do exist are often of poor quality. Thus, in rural areas, key MDGs relating to infant, child and maternal mortality have not been met (The World Bank, 2017). It is also notable that early childbirth declined only slightly over the period, and one in seven women still have their first child before the age of 18 (Male and Wodon, 2016).

Since 2005, the *Juntos* conditional cash transfer programme has provided additional social security, and childhood outcomes have improved (The World Bank, 2017). As with the other Young Lives countries, education and nutrition are important government priorities. With primary school enrolment nearly universal and net enrolment in secondary education increasing, policy attention has focused on addressing inequalities in access to tertiary education, policy coordination, and the challenges young people face in an informal labour market. A National Secretariat of Youth was established in 2011 and concentrates on educational access, employment and healthcare (Rojas et al, 2016). A cross-sectoral National Plan of Action for Children and Adolescents for 2012-21 brings together actions to drive integrated improvements in adolescents' lives.

Vietnam represents a remarkable development story, having risen within a generation from 20 years of conflict (1955-75). Strong and equitable economic growth and access to basic services have reduced the percentage of the population living in extreme poverty to almost zero and the (higher) national income poverty rate from 21% in 2010 to 10% in 2016 (Pimhidzai, 2018). In addition, health and education outcomes have improved rapidly (Eckardt et al, 2016). Between 2005 and 2015, Vietnam's urban population rose steeply from 23 million to 31 million (UN Habitat, 2016). The rapid expansion of mobile telephony and internet access reflects accelerated technological change. The Vietnamese education system is increasingly being cited as an example of excellence by other countries, particularly because of the impressive results in the Programme for International Student Assessment (OECD, 2016).

Although there has been progress recently for the poorest communities (Pimhidzai, 2018), stark differences still exist between the circumstances of the ethnic majority groups and ethnic minorities: many of the latter live in relatively remote, mountainous areas and experience significant ongoing disadvantages, including higher rates of poverty. Livelihoods remain fragile, and while Vietnam has established wide health insurance coverage (legislation adopted in 2009 created a national programme), social assistance is much more limited. Narrowing the welfare gap between Vietnam's ethnic majority and minority groups has been a government priority, including through area-based development schemes, such as Programme 135, which aims to accelerate production and promote market-oriented agricultural development, reduce poverty and improve socio-cultural life among ethnic groups in impoverished areas. Nevertheless, secondary school drop-out rates and under-nutrition continue to be high among minority communities. Vietnam has a low fertility rate and is on its way to becoming one of the world's most rapidly ageing societies, as the demographic dividend supported by its economic transformation dissipates (Eckardt et al, 2016). Enhancing productivity by ensuring the supply of skilled labour is thus increasingly important to Vietnam's continued development, as set out in the Socio-Economic Development Plan 2016-2020 (Socialist Republic of Vietnam, 2016), and the effectiveness of the education and training systems is receiving considerable attention.

How evidence is used in this book

As a longitudinal observational study of children that spans the first two decades of life, Young Lives is well positioned to track children's developmental trajectories across the early life course.

The design permits analytic techniques to untangle the complex relationship between poverty and child outcomes, also showing how direct, moderating, mediating and transactional processes influence these outcomes through the points in development covered by the data collection rounds. Young Lives evidence reveals this multidimensionality and identifies the most important processes that shape children's later development. The diversity of the sample also highlights the differences in wellbeing and development between boys and girls from different social and economic groups growing up in different places and in four different countries.

This book relies on many underlying studies created by researchers working on the Young Lives data as well as original analysis completed for the book. Where statistics and narratives from interviews are quoted without attribution to a specific source, these are derived either from analysis of Young Lives data undertaken for the book or descriptive patterns published on the Young Lives website.[4]

Young Lives was set up to examine children's experiences and what matters for their development and wellbeing. The study followed children, rather than tracking changes in policies or their implementation in the study sites. And so the evidence is most informative in understanding what the challenges are to improving children's life chances. To bring the Young Lives evidence together with the policy evaluation literature, the book makes use of evidence from evaluations and systematic reviews of interventions for children in a wide range of LMICs. Many of these are drawn from the impressive 3iE database and have been vetted for quality.[5] Systematic reviews apply strict inclusion criteria and these often exclude qualitative studies and information in the 'grey' literature from non-governmental organisations and others that do not always evaluate or publish evidence about programmes in ways that meet prescribed standards. This approach underlines the quality of programme evaluation, but we recognise that it might also omit some important knowledge.

Structure of the book

The structure of this book reflects the life course approach used in Young Lives research, which also largely follows the logic defined by Bundy and colleagues (2018), who identify the first 8,000 days of life (from conception to about 21 years) as the most critical period for human development. The main empirical chapters of the book are aligned with the different phases of this period: infancy and early childhood, middle childhood, adolescence and youth. Findings from

Young Lives are synthesised and the policy implications discussed in the framework thus created, although it is recognised that the evidence shared in particular chapters often goes beyond the specific life phase addressed in that chapter.

Chapter Two outlines the Young Lives study design and conceptualisation, and introduces the bioecological framework that guides Young Lives research and analysis. This framework provides a way to consider how the nested environments around children – such as family, community, and society – influence their lives. Recognising that successive pressures and protective factors in these environments can have cumulative effects, the chapter also introduces the concept of a developmental cascade, which facilitates detection of what matters most for children in different life phases and shows how multiple influences may either undermine or enhance children's development and wellbeing.

Chapter Three highlights some of the major social and economic trends in the Young Lives study countries over the past 15 years and briefly indicates how such trends have affected and are perceived by sample children, their caregivers and households. Chapters Four, Five and Six follow a life course approach by addressing children's development during the three major phases of childhood – early childhood, middle childhood and adolescence and youth – in turn. Evidence is presented in each chapter of what matters most during each life phase. Early care is a particular focus of Chapter Four, education of Chapter Five, and the growing importance of work and social relationships in Chapter Six. The chapters trace the early determinants of a series of subsequent consequences for children's physical development, learning, cognition and psychosocial wellbeing, as well as the different perspectives of children and their educators on these aspects of their lives.

Chapter Seven brings together data on the life phases to address what matters most and when in children's lives. This analysis is made possible by the nature of Young Lives data, and benefits from the use of the same research instruments over time across the four countries. This approach follows the logic of the developmental cascade to consider how children's cognitive achievement 'grows' across the life course, and what helped or hindered this development. Chapter Eight summarises key messages and reflects on what has been learned from running the Young Lives study.

Notes

[1] The names of individuals and communities have been changed to protect their anonymity.

[2]   www.census2011.co.in/states.php

[3]   Scheduled Tribes refers to specific indigenous peoples whose status has been formally acknowledged in government regulations as different from other religious and socio-cultural groups. Scheduled Caste is the official name given to the 'lowest' (and socially most disadvantaged) caste. 'Other backward class' is a term used for groups that are socially, educationally or economically disadvantaged, but not by caste.

[4]   See www.younglives.org.uk/content/round-5-fact-sheets and other sources on the Young Lives website.

[5]   www.3ieimpact.org/en/evidence/systematic-reviews

TWO

The Young Lives design and conceptual framework

This chapter outlines the Young Lives study design and conceptual framework. It explains how the framework is used to build an understanding of the ways in which poverty affects children's development and wellbeing. The chapter begins by describing the key methodological features of Young Lives and their utility for policy insight. This is followed by a discussion of how Young Lives perceives child development, highlighting the bioecological life course framework that underpins this view. The chapter concludes with a description of the implications of exposure to poverty and other risks for children's development and wellbeing throughout their lives, using the idea of a developmental cascade, which provides a tool to inform policies and programmes, as outlined in subsequent chapters of the book.

Study design and relevance for policy

The sample

Young Lives is a unique comparative, mixed-methods longitudinal study of approximately 12,000 boys and girls growing up in Ethiopia, United Andhra Pradesh in India, Peru and Vietnam. The children are divided into two age groups, roughly 4,000 'Older Cohort' children born around 1994 and enrolled at 8 years, and about 8,000 'Younger Cohort' children born around 2001 and enrolled at between 6 and 18 months, or approximately age 1.[1] Children were sampled randomly from 80 rural and urban sentinel sites – 20 in each study country. The study is broadly pro-poor, insofar as more affluent areas were excluded in all four countries.[2] The sample is now more dispersed due to migration, and the formation of new families and households by Older Cohort participants.

One of the chief reasons for the perpetuation of child poverty and inequality is the exclusion of communities, households and children from the services, resources and wider benefits of the societies in which they live. Thus, the study sample is intentionally varied, the aim being to collect data from children in different communities and populations, and to produce findings that are broadly representative of the diversity of social groups in each country, but not necessarily nationally representative. The sample comprises equal numbers of boys and girls and is very varied in terms of rural and urban location, household economic status, and membership of social, religious, ethnic and language groups, and in India, castes. Information gathered simultaneously across four countries makes it possible to identify commonalities and differences not only within, but also between, the national samples, ensuring that the findings are relevant to the study-countries and to other contexts. By interviewing the children regularly as they grow up, the study has been able to identify clear developmental and wellbeing disparities between the different groups and show how these manifest during different life stages.

Research methods and data

Young Lives gathers data using multiple distinct, but interrelated components. The four main tools are: household-based surveys with children, caregivers and community representatives; longitudinal qualitative research with children and caregivers; school effectiveness surveys; and qualitative sub-studies on focused topics. The design ensures that the different components are complementary and feed into the whole: survey findings give rise to topics for in-depth qualitative study, while data from the latter inform questions for subsequent survey rounds. For example, in India it was established through the survey that many children were attending private schools, and this led to a sub-study examining what lies behind school choice.

Detailed survey data collected since 2002 cover a wide range of topics, including children's perspectives, attitudes, hopes and aspirations, as well as time use, health and cognitive skills, and psychosocial wellbeing. In 2007, a longitudinal qualitative research component with a subsample of 200 of the children – 100 from each of the two age cohorts – was added. These data allow for a deeper look at the themes addressed in the survey, such as children's experiences and perspectives on poverty, their hopes for the future and their views on school and work. Methods included semi-structured interviews, observation, drawing and focus groups.

Findings from the early survey rounds revealed how central schooling was to the aspirations of the children and their families. Yet, it was also apparent that some of the children were not progressing well. School surveys were thus introduced in 2010 to investigate influences of school factors on learning outcomes. This investigation was conducted with two waves of school-effectiveness surveys at primary and secondary level and involved nearly 30,000 children in schools attended by Young Lives children and their peers. The design entailed measurement of many age-appropriate indicators of school performance, including curricula-aligned tests of mathematics and language abilities, and psychosocial wellbeing. Tests were administered at the start and end of the school year to track progress.

In recent years further sub-studies have been introduced, and they provide detailed information on context-specific topics, including children's work, social protection, early marriage, parenthood, and sexual and reproductive health. Figure 2.1 sets out the overall design of the study.

Data are available on both cohorts at three age points (8, 12 and 15 years). This feature allows analysis over time, by comparing the cohorts. Data were also collected on the younger siblings of the Younger Cohort to enable intra-household analysis.

The Young Lives mixed-method approach combines the power of statistics with the depth of qualitative analysis. Much of the evidence on children's wellbeing and development is derived from questionnaires administered to caregivers and children, often using internationally

Figure 2.1: Young Lives study design

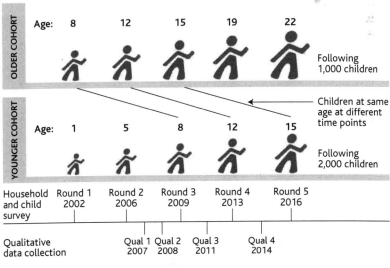

recognised instruments. In addition to foregrounding children's experiences, the qualitative component facilitates explanation of trends identified through the surveys. For example, evidence about children's education aspirations, along with the experiences of boys and girls of schooling, work and domestic life, is combined with information about their attainment through school and learning outcomes.

Longitudinal cohort data of the kind collected by Young Lives are particularly useful for policy because they paint a picture of the pathways by which disadvantage is transmitted across the life course and, in the case of Young Lives, also between generations. The kind of multipurpose cohort design underpinning the study is more frequently employed in high-income than in low- and middle-income countries (LMICs), where longitudinal research has tended to focus on health or nutrition. The Consortium of Health-Orientated Research in Transitioning Societies, which comprises Pelotas in Brazil, the New Delhi Birth Cohort in India, the Cebu Longitudinal Health and Nutrition Survey cohort in the Philippines, the Institute of Nutrition of Central America and Panama Nutrition Trial Cohort in Guatemala, and Birth-to-Twenty in South Africa, is the most prominent network of cohort studies in LMICs (Richter et al, 2012). This group has shown the benefit of comparative analysis by pooling data from diverse countries and cohorts, and by doing so, has offered compelling evidence on the importance of early childhood interventions. Young Lives builds on this tradition and experience. Uniquely, Young Lives has gathered information simultaneously from a large sample of two age cohorts living in four countries.

The findings reported in this book rely on analyses of the qualitative and quantitative data generated by the study. A well-recognised problem with observational (that is, non-experimental) data in longitudinal studies is that while associations can be established, these links may be overestimated, and the relationships may not be causal (Bailey et al, 2017). Young Lives is not an experimental study and so cannot establish cause in the manner of a randomised controlled trial, sometimes regarded as the 'gold standard' for informing programme recommendations – assuming that the findings can be generalised to other contexts.

Care is taken in this book not to attribute cause from correlational data, but any instances where the relationship is strong and plausibly a causal one (on the basis of the analytical procedure, other evidence and theory) are indicated (Pearl, 2012). Young Lives has collected a wide range of variables likely to influence children's outcomes over the course of development. This approach increases the possibility of controlling for multiple effects. Apart from the design and the rich set of variables available, analytic techniques used in the studies referenced here include quasi-experimental approaches (group comparisons), multiple regression and latent growth modelling (LGM), among others. LGM provides an empirical test of a plausible theoretical model of how predictors influence developmental change.[3] When the same relationships are observed across children's development in each of the four countries, the external validity of the findings is evident. These characteristics make it appropriate to draw out implications for policy. Specific recommendations for specific interventions (for example, to improve literacy outcomes) cannot be provided by Young Lives data alone, since these do require experimental evidence. But the findings paint a broader picture and can certainly indicate where there is a need for policy and interventions to address particular issues – the specific nature of these interventions may need to be decided on the basis of proven programmes, if these are available, or such programmes developed and tested. These implications are strengthened in this book by reference to systematic reviews of studies following experimental approaches.

Sample attrition

In longitudinal research there are always concerns that the sample may diminish with time (termed attrition). If some groups are more likely than others to be lost to the sample, findings may be biased. Table 2.1 shows the Young Lives attrition rate, this being the percentage of the children who were originally recruited into the study and who had left it by the time of the fifth survey round in 2016. Annualising the latest figures in the table shows that attrition is typically much less than 1% per year. Reasons for leaving the study vary and include refusal to participate in later rounds, and failure to trace those who have migrated. Deaths are not included in attrition rates since they are

Table 2.1: Attrition and death rates between 2002 and 2016 (% of the 2002 sample)

	Younger Cohort		Older Cohort	
	Attrition	Deaths	Attrition	Deaths
Ethiopia	5.3	4.3	17.7	1.1
India (UAP)	3.7	2.3	7.6	1.7
Peru	8.2	1.2	14.1	0.8
Vietnam	2.5	0.7	8.6	0.3

a research finding, and not a measure of data quality.[4] Sadly, though, several children from the original sample have died since the study's inception. Deaths have been highest among the Younger Cohort in Ethiopia, the poorest of the four countries, and among the poorest children generally (Sánchez and Escobal, forthcoming).[5]

Attrition is considerably lower in Young Lives than a range of comparable studies (assessed by Sánchez and Escobal, forthcoming). This is largely due to significant efforts by the country teams to track, and maintain trust and contact with participants. Strategies include retaining the same field supervisors across the rounds whenever possible, and maintaining effective links with study communities and regular contact with participants who have moved. Attrition is higher in the Older Cohort than in the Younger Cohort, possibly because the older group were more likely to have moved away from their birth home or community by the fifth survey round (Sánchez and Escobal, forthcoming).[6]

The Young Lives conceptual framework

Young Lives conceptualisation of child development

Young Lives follows the definition of childhood provided in the United Nations Convention on the Rights of the Child, which refers to all individuals below age 18 as children. That said, the study accepts that while this definition is widely used, it is not always a perfect fit with social designations in which chronological criteria may have a limited role. There are age overlaps in commonly used definitions of early and middle childhood, adolescence and youth. In the Young Lives research the 'early childhood' phase refers to 0-5 years and 'middle childhood' to the period from 6 to 12 years. Following World Health Organization practice (Patton et al, 2016), 'adolescence' is defined as encompassing ages 10 to 19 years (with early adolescence from 10-14 years and late adolescence from 15-19 years). 'Youth' indicates transitional phase through early adulthood, covering roughly ages 15-24 years. In the context of education research and policy specifically, Young Lives uses the institutional terms of preschool, and primary, secondary and tertiary education and training.

The Young Lives design builds on an understanding of human development as a lifelong process, which in the case of children and adolescents focuses on the 'acquisition and growth of the physical, cognitive, social and emotional competencies required to engage fully in family and society' (Aber et al, 1997, p 47). This definition highlights how development includes multiple functional domains, each comprising a set of states and skills that interact and influence all other aspects of development, so that, for example, physical health affects cognition and learning. Analysing the links across such developmental domains over time allows the study to show how deprivations in one area of development (such as growth stunting) may affect others (such as neurological development), with cumulative impact (for example, limited cognitive abilities leading to poor school performance and eventual drop-out).

Human development is the product of complex transactions between individual action, genotypic biological and physiological maturation processes, and the external context (Sameroff, 2009; Shonkoff, 2010). Acknowledging that many factors shape human development raises the question of whether differences in children's abilities, such as the school performance of children from different socioeconomic backgrounds, are likely to be primarily a function of differences in genetic endowment or environment, in this case economic status. For instance, an argument could be made that poor people are in poverty, at least in part because of their genetic make-up and its association with limited abilities, and that parents pass these traits on to their children. Children may not perform poorly due to poor learning environments, but rather because they are less well endowed with cognitive potential than their wealthier counterparts. However, the neuroscientific study of child poverty and epigenetics rejects this determinist argument (Lipina and Segretin, 2015). The role of the environment in influencing gene expression across the life cycle is increasingly evident (Lenroot and Giedd, 2011).

Although studies have established that cognitive skills are heritable (Kovas et al, 2007; Haworth et al, 2009), observed abilities are a function of the interaction of children's potentials and their learning environments, which contribute substantially to differences in observed abilities (Davis et al, 2014). Similarly, research on the effects of participation in well-designed preschool programmes in low-income countries show that children from poor backgrounds gain significant benefit (Nores and Barnett, 2010; Rao et al, 2012). Young Lives research in Vietnamese primary schools is consistent with this conclusion (see Chapter Five). In the United States, increases in family income in early and middle childhood lead to higher reading and mathematics abilities. Such effects are significantly greater for lower income children than for their wealthier counterparts because more of their potential is otherwise compromised (Dahl and Lochner, 2005; Duncan et al, 2010).

A bioecological life course framework

Young Lives conceives of the processes of human development as being shaped by more proximal (for example, family) and distal (for example, the national economy) contexts. The study also recognises the critical role of young people in influencing their own development. These relationships are set out in the bioecological approach to the study of human development that guides the Young Lives conceptualisation. This framework shows changeable influences operating at different levels in society, affecting different aspects of human development in different life phases. This approach draws heavily on the work of Urie Bronfenbrenner and others (for example, Bronfenbrenner and Morris, 2006) and is shown in Figure 2.2.

In the bioecological framework the 'context' for human development is a system of nested and interdependent structures operating at levels close to or further from the child, as Figure 2.2 shows. As children proceed beyond early childhood, through middle childhood, adolescence and youth, they bring dispositions and capacities developed earlier to new contexts, and in which there are other people. The role of family members may remain important, but the influence of schools, teachers and peers increases (Brechwald and Prinstein, 2011). The most proximal and intimate level (the microsystem) comprises enduring relationships with caregivers, school teachers and peers, who exercise a direct impact on children's development through relationship formation, learning of shared norms and values, and participation

Figure 2.2: Bioecological life course framework

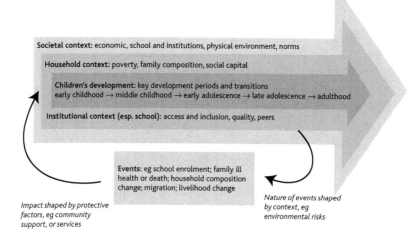

Societal context: economic, school and institutions, physical environment, norms

Household context: poverty, family composition, social capital

Children's development: key development periods and transitions
early childhood → middle childhood → early adolescence → late adolescence → adulthood

Institutional context (esp. school): access and inclusion, quality, peers

Events: eg school enrolment; family ill health or death; household composition change; migration; livelihood change

Impact shaped by protective factors, eg community support, or services

Nature of events shaped by context, eg environmental risks

in routine activities (Rogoff, 2003). The family context also affects children's development through its influence on their engagement with external systems (mesosystems in Bronfenbrenner's model) such as the school, for example when family poverty undermines school attainment. Also important are the settings that affect the people who are in close relationships with the child. For example, families living in dangerous neighbourhoods may exercise restrictive control over children, particularly girls, out of fear for their safety and risks to their reputations (Pinderhughes et al, 2001).

The human and physical characteristics of the child's community exert increasing influence as children move beyond the home to play, work, attend school and join social groups (Furstenberg and Hughes, 1997). The natural and built environments are vital constituents at this level. Environmental stressors, including physical hazards such as unsafe housing or traffic, and environmental degradation in the form of water, air and land pollution, as well as wider climate change, operate in numerous ways to threaten children. Thus, for example, exposure to toxic environments, whether because of human activity such as urban congestion or extreme weather events such as drought, impairs brain and physical development. Poor sanitation and environmental toxins, including lead exposure, air pollution (Brims and Chauhan, 2005) and noise pollution (Clark et al, 2006), can have lifelong consequences for health, learning, behaviour and achievement (Gavidia et al, 2009).

The most distal set of influences in Bronfenbrenner's model (the macro system) includes those that shape all other systems. Though this 'context' is often set aside as important but difficult to measure, macro-system structures and processes significantly affect children's wellbeing and development. These have their origins in national policies, in economic conditions, in social and institutional structures and in widely held cultural values and attitudes, as well as in the quality of and sustained access to natural and manufactured resources. Many of these factors are discussed in Chapter Three. Such influences substantially determine both advantage and disadvantage, affecting children through their household circumstances. For example, the economic and social circumstances of caregivers, and their preferences, decisions and actions, are particularly important in early childhood (Shonkoff, 2010; Wachs and Rahman, 2013), a finding reinforced in Chapter Seven. Other macro-system influences such as labour market opportunities and droughts or floods or other shocks will have consequences across age points. Socio-cultural factors may also result in discrimination against ethnic minority group children or members of particular castes in the education system, thereby reducing opportunities to learn and progress.

Finally, there is a dynamic relationship between human development and the changing nature of external influences over time, processes and outcomes that Young Lives is able to illuminate with its two cohort cross-sequential design, where children are measured at the same ages but at different points in time. This relationship is crucial to a child's development, as exposure to adversity can have different effects at different stages of life and multiple adversities over time can have cumulative effects. On the other hand, some children may be able to overcome disadvantages, and go from strength to strength. This dynamic process has been characterised by the concept of a 'developmental cascade' (Masten and Cicchetti, 2010, p 491):

> Developmental cascades refer to the cumulative consequences for development of the many interactions and transactions occurring in developing systems that result in spreading effects across levels, among domains at the same level, and across different systems or generations ... developmental cascades alter the course of development.

The concept of a developmental cascade allows for operationalisation of the bioecological framework over time, as it indicates how the factors working at the micro, meso and macro levels affect children's development as they grow. Thus, cascades operate within particular periods of development, as when growth stunting in the first 1,000 days of life – typically caused by under-nutrition and poor health – compromises neurological development, in turn affecting cognitive functioning and schooling. Cascades also operate across phases of development, as when early outcomes have cumulative effects across the full life cycle. While poverty leads generally to negative cascades, positive cascades are possible also, where benefits accumulate across the life course. For example, children who have received supportive care and form a secure attachment to a caregiver are more likely to trust others and find it relatively easy to develop good relationships with peers at school and beyond.

Sensitive periods of development

Young Lives research examines children's development over two decades of life, drawing attention to the trajectories and transitions children go through as they grow up. This life course approach reveals how early circumstances relate to later outcomes, breaking down what happens within individual lives, to examine what matters most for whom, and when it matters. In some respects, human development follows universal and predictable patterns, whether driven by universal biological growth processes, or by culturally shaped regularities such as the passage through education, which in most countries involves progression through age grades. In other respects, development varies widely according to context, as when children who work learn pro-social skills well in advance of their schooled peers. There are sensitive developmental periods when the pace, scale and complexity of change is accelerated and sensitivity to external influences increases. Key social, cultural and institutional transitions, such as puberty rites, or the transition from primary to secondary school, may also heighten responsiveness to external stimuli. Sensitive periods are important in policy discussions, since they highlight 'windows of opportunity' for intervention.

Recently, the period lasting until 1,000 days after conception has come to be recognised as the critical period of foetal and infant vulnerability, especially in light of the loss of 'developmental potential' due to poverty and other stressors during this phase (Grantham-McGregor et al, 2007). *In utero* deprivation, such as maternal under-nutrition, chronic stress and substance abuse, affect the development of the foetus (see, for example, Liu, 2011). Health, nutrition and learning opportunities during the earliest months and years shape the developing brain in ways that enable or compromise the neurological architecture required for the development and expression of motor, language, cognitive and socio-emotional skills (Grantham-McGregor et al, 2007), all of which are required for effective participation in the household, the school and ultimately the workplace. The evidence is clear that in early childhood, the quality of the care environment plays a crucial role in the development of capacities that are central to health, learning, and social and emotional functioning.

Middle childhood is a time when crucial pro-social competencies, such as confidence, social connection and caring (Lerner et al, 2000), are developed in critically important contexts, including schools, families and peer networks. This is also when many children begin to combine school with work, both of which offer opportunities for the development of new skills, as well as engagement with individuals and groups outside the family, especially peers. These activities can also pose new challenges and may entail certain risks. For example, schools may either compensate for the effects of early childhood poverty and exclusion through high-quality provision or compound a negative cascade with poor teaching and resources (Hoadley, 2013).

There is increasing recognition that adolescence is another sensitive period for development and wellbeing. Significant changes in physical, neurological and psychosocial development occur during adolescence and these often have consequences for transitions to adulthood (UNICEF, 2011; WHO, 2014a; Patton et al, 2016). Biological changes in early adolescence such as puberty also have cultural significance, triggering gendered changes in status, responsibilities and expectations.

The Young Lives Older Cohort has been followed up to 22 years of age, which in this book is included in the period called 'youth' (Hardgrove et al, 2014). Youth has emerged as a distinct life phase relatively recently as societies develop economies requiring extended periods of education and training, resulting in longer periods of dependency on kin, later entry to the labour force and delayed family formation (Klein, 1990). Youth is marked by social transitions such as moving into further education and training, taking up full-time paid work, and starting a family, important moments of change associated with heightened vulnerability, but also opportunities for growth (Morrow, 2013a; Roest, 2016).

Child poverty

Since Young Lives is primarily concerned with understanding how children's development is shaped by poverty and inequality, children's experiences of and responses to material shortfalls and associated adversities are at its core. The Young Lives conceptualisation of poverty is multidimensional and signifies a level of material and social resources and service access that is insufficient to ensure healthy development and wellbeing, and effective participation in society. However, analyses of the survey data use a more restrictive definition – children living in households with relatively low material living standards, as assessed through a 'wealth index', which is a composite measure comprising access to services, consumer durables and housing conditions (described in Briones, 2017).[7] Recent Young Lives publications identify the poorest children as those living in the bottom third of households ranked according to this index, a convention that is followed in this book, unless otherwise stated. This measure is intentionally focused on material indicators of wealth and can be used to identify links to other aspects of life, such as levels of health, education, or the quality of a child's environment, and social connectedness both at a household level and within the wider community (Dornan and Boyden, 2011). Poverty is itself associated with other forms of adversity, such as dwelling in marginal locations that are prone to pollution or extreme weather events, and the study can track the cumulative effect on children of exposure to such co-occurring risks.

Understood as another major source of hazard to children, inequality is taken to involve hierarchy, as manifested in differences in access to services, material and social resources, as well as in children's outcomes (Dornan and Woodhead, 2015). These disparities may be due to either economic differences between individuals and households (generally measured through economic criteria such as the gini coefficient), or differences between social groups, based on their ethnicity, religion, language, gender or other criteria (see Stewart, 2000). Where group-based social inequalities intersect with inequalities in individual or household wealth, this can compound and reinforce poverty (Kabeer, 2016).

Risk and resilience

The complexity of the bioecological system, and its processes and structures, means that outcomes of early experience are probabilistic rather than deterministic. Children exposed to the same trauma or hazard may react very differently, with variable consequences. The concepts 'vulnerability' and 'resilience' are often used to convey the different ways in which humans respond to adversity individually (Luthar et al, 2000; Masten, 2001). For most researchers, resilience denotes good outcomes despite misfortune. Resilience may in part be an inherent characteristic of the individual – either due to biological make-up, or to ability to cope with adverse circumstances. However, the term 'resilience' also acknowledges the extent to which children's circumstances – such as household and community support, and access to services – include protective buffers that moderate the impact of adverse events on them (Zolkoski and Bullock, 2012; Wachs and Rahman, 2013).

Individual variations in exposure to environmental risks, opportunities for resilience building and support, and genetic make-up, all affect children's trajectories. While it is critical to draw attention to early risks, it is essential also to 'avoid the assumption that only early risks are critical or that early interventions can act as an inoculation against all later risks' (Wachs and Rahman, 2013, p 86). Insults occurring later can have long-term adverse effects just as protective factors can promote recovery from certain forms of early adversity. In this light, longitudinal research shows the importance of early life events, and also offsets concerns about the irreversibility of early shocks, identifying the potential for recovery through remedial interventions and other means (Alderman and Walker, 2014; Georgiadis, 2016).

Conclusion

The work of Young Lives is underpinned by a number of key principles. Child development is fundamentally shaped by the national, community and family contexts in which children live, and by the relationships within which skills, beliefs and wellbeing are fostered. Child development involves a complex transaction between individual action, genotypic, biological and physiological maturation processes, and external contextual influences, such that changes in the child and in the context in which he or she lives are both dynamic and mutually constitutive. Fully understanding children's development through the life course requires a broad framework that includes attention to the many structures and processes affecting caregivers, families, and households, as these in turn affect children. The child-context interface has very different effects on development at different ages, depending on features of the child and her or his position in the wider society. Hence economic status, gender and other social markers such as ethnicity may determine resource allocation, treatment and opportunities that vary in influence at different points in the life course. However, the outcomes of early experience are probabilistic rather than deterministic, and children's development may be tipped towards either a negative or positive developmental cascade, depending on the balance of protective influences and risks and their varying effects over time.

The bioecological model provides the core conceptual basis for the study, identifying the many layers and influences on children's development, and encouraging an analysis of how those wider structural determinants shape poverty and inequalities facing children. Since the cascade approach helps explain how advantages and disadvantages accumulate, it provides a policy tool to assess the factors that make the greatest difference for which children and at which point in their lives.

Notes

[1]   There are roughly 1,000 children in the Older Cohort and 2,000 in the Younger Cohort in each country, with slightly fewer Older Cohort children in Peru.

[2]   The sample has been compared with nationally representative data by Escobal and Flores (2008); Kumra (2008); Nguyen (2008); and Outes-Leon and Sánchez (2008).

3 Latent growth modelling is developed and presented in Chapter Seven. Given the novelty of the approach, methodological detail is provided in the chapter and in a separate working paper (Tredoux and Dawes, 2018).

4 In the Older Cohort, more boys died than girls. For the Younger Cohort, in all countries but Vietnam, slightly more girls than boys died. The differences between the rates of deaths of boys and girls tend to be small and are not statistically significant.

5 The probability of high infant mortality in a pro-poor sample was the main reason why the Younger Cohort was recruited after participants had already reached six months of age.

6 Sánchez and Escobal (forthcoming) find no evidence of attrition bias for the Younger Cohort, but some bias for the Older Cohort. Household socioeconomic status was linked to attrition, but there was no consistent pattern across the countries of which children were more likely to be lost to attrition.

7 A fuller multidimensional measure (combining health, education, material and other circumstances) would be inappropriate as combining inputs and outcomes would limit the potential to explore relationships between variables.

THREE

Growing up in a time of extraordinary change

The Young Lives children have grown up during a period of rapid economic, social and policy change. The bioecological model points to the importance of this national and community context in shaping the circumstances facing children directly or via the household. This chapter highlights how living standards and access to basic services have improved across the study period. It shows that Young Lives children enjoy better circumstances than did their parents when they were young, and also that many aspects of life are better for the Younger Cohort than they were for the Older Cohort at the same ages. Changes in access to education between the generations are particularly dramatic. The rise of education around the world is changing norms, with modern childhood becoming increasingly synonymous with schooling. While access to basic services in the four countries clearly improved over the study period, risks and shocks remained common, particularly in rural areas. And while children in cities and towns were often doing better than those in rural areas, parents' accounts highlighted concerns over new risks facing children.

The current generation of children is doing much better than previous generations

Young Lives has traced children's evolving circumstances by assessing household wealth, caregiver situation, and community infrastructure and services regularly at each survey round. Rapid economic growth has led to real changes for Young Lives children, households and communities. These changes have largely been for the better. Levels of poverty have reduced, access to infrastructure and services has expanded, children enjoy better housing conditions, and families report owning more durables such as radios and bicycles.

The pace of change has been extraordinary. This is evident from the case of Latha, who lives in Katur, a rural village in the Rayalaseema region of United Andhra Pradesh. The area is prone to drought, with high levels of seasonal out-migration. In 2014, Latha and her mother discussed how life had changed. Fewer people live in desperate poverty; and social protection schemes and self-help groups have raised wages and reduced the number of people who migrate for work (Pells and Woodhead, 2014). Latha says families' dependence on powerful local interests has decreased:

> Then, people used to go for work for Reddy [a socially and economically powerful landowning caste] households ... they only had food only if we worked for them, madam. Otherwise our stomachs were empty.... Now, it's not like that. (Interview transcript)

Her mother is clear that Latha's life has been better than her own: 'She has not undergone the sufferings and pain as I had gone through.' She explains that water and electricity supplies have improved women's daily lives:

> Those days there was no electricity, there was no street taps and water. For water we used to go to wells and fetch water, there were no plastic pots, we used to buy the mud pots and use to get water with them. She [Latha] never went so far for water, as I had gone. They had put up a borehole and the village Sarpanch won the elections so he had put these taps. (Interview transcript)

> In those days, we had to grind everything manually in the grinding stones every day, then we had to prepare *roti*. There was no electricity, we have [sic] to depend on kerosene lamps, now they have electricity, machines. Now to prepare food, you just take the rice and wash and cook it, that's it. (Interview transcript)

The inhabitants of Katur can now catch a bus by walking to the main road, and motorised rickshaws have started coming right into the village. Access to health services has improved, even if people still have to travel for treatment, and few women give birth at home. Few Young Lives mothers in rural areas went to school. Latha's mother reported: 'I never stepped through the entrance of the school' (interview transcript). At the age of 5 or so, she and her siblings would stay alone at home while their parents worked, and by early adolescence, she was working in the fields as an agricultural labourer. In common with many of the Young Lives caregivers, she says attitudes to education have transformed, including attitudes to girls' schooling:

Now the girls are studying. Those days there was no school and no one showed an interest in education. Now everyone wants to study so that they will get one or the other job.... At least they may live happily, and they need not lead a donkey's life as we had lived. (Interview transcript)

Across the study many Young Lives families reported improved access to electricity, water, and other basic services, with important benefits for children's nutrition, study, workloads, health and dignity. One way of showing just how much better the lives of the current generation of children are than the lives of previous generations is by comparing the outcomes of the Young Lives children with those of their caregivers. For example, significant progress in health, nutrition and service access is shown by the fact that the average 22-year-old girl in the Older Cohort is taller than her mother by 2.5 centimetres in United Andhra Pradesh, 4.6 centimetres in Peru, and 3.6 centimetres in Vietnam.[1] The gains in Peru are particularly striking, but they are consistent across the countries, although in Ethiopia the gains are small.

Nearly all Young Lives children enrolled in school for a significant portion of the study period. The majority stayed at school well into their teenage years, extending childhood and opening up a period of adolescence between childhood and adulthood. Figure 3.1 shows that a high proportion of the Older Cohort had more education than their parents, the most dramatic disparity being between mothers and daughters, suggesting a narrowing of gendered inequalities. The differences were especially large in Ethiopia and United Andhra Pradesh.

Expanded school access has often been widely welcomed by children and families as allowing young people to access better jobs. Educational expansion is also associated with extraordinarily high education aspirations among Young Lives children and caregivers, even if realities often do not live up to hopes. When the Younger Cohort children were aged 12 years, the majority of their caregivers – 81% in Peru, 77% in Ethiopia, 75% in Vietnam and 73% in United Andhra Pradesh – aspired for them to reach tertiary education. Young Lives caregivers certainly associate expanded school access with many improvements in the children's lives. One Young Lives aunt, a rural to urban migrant in Vietnam, said: 'Compared with my niece's situation now, it is a great difference, as different as is the heaven from the earth ... I had to struggle to survive, otherwise I could not

Figure 3.1: Primary and secondary school enrolment for the Older Cohort by age 22 compared with that of their parents (%)

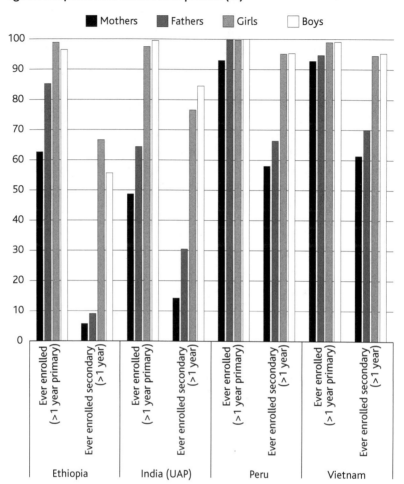

exist' (interview transcript). The grandmother of a girl in Ethiopia commented:

> During our time, we were unable to decide on our life, but today children have the right to decide. If parents attempt to marry them without their permission, they will sue their parents.... Children today are very much wise.... Her life will definitely be good because she will be educated and may even marry someone who is educated. (Interview transcript)

Above all, across very different contexts school is seen as both an exit route from poverty and manual labour and the marker of a decent life:

> We did not know that education was very important as we do now ... Adugna's life is better than mine. For one thing, he is learning with freedom; he has time to go to school. We did not have time and girls were not attending school in our area. When I compare my life with that of Adugna, the difference is like the sky and the earth. (Adugna's mother, Ethiopia, quoted in Crivello and van der Gaag, 2016, p 17)

> We remained ignorant and we don't want our children also like that. We lived our lives eating porridge and gathering firewood. Now the times have changed. ... We are getting them educated so that they will have decent and good life. (Preethi's mother, tribal area, United Andhra Pradesh; interview transcript)

For the Older Cohort girls, remaining in school is associated with later transitions to marriage, cohabitation and childbearing, reflecting global trends (UNICEF, 2018). For example, Latha's mother got married three years after she reached menarche, whereas Latha had reached 20 before she married. Her mother reflected that girls these days have a – somewhat – greater say about marriage.

> We could not oppose what elders used to say, we had to obey them. We could not tell them 'I will not get married.' Nowadays they ask the girl whether they like the boy or not. (Interview transcript)

Latha works hard in her in-laws' house but gets along well with her husband. She says: 'I am lucky to have a husband I like' (interview transcript). Her husband and brother-in-law make her laugh, and her sister-in-law helps her with housework. Her mother-in-law 'won't direct [me] to do [my work] this way or that way ... she only says "Do it as you like"' (interview transcript). By 2016, aged 22, Latha had one daughter and was pregnant for a second time.

In Ethiopia, some of the mothers and grandmothers of Young Lives children who themselves suffered by marrying too young have played a part in changing attitudes and practices towards girls' education and marriage. Haftey, an orphan, was raised by her grandmother. The grandmother grew up in a village without a school and her parents arranged for her to marry when she was aged just nine. The marriage lasted for only a short time. The grandmother explained that this was because she was too young to be married. When asked 'Would you have liked to have gone to school?', she replied: 'Who knows? I didn't have any idea…. School was not known at that time….' She was remarried when she was in her mid-teens. This was a happier marriage and the couple had nine children. But, tragically, seven of the children died while still quite young – including Haftey's mother. The grandmother attributed her children's deaths to her poverty and lack of experience, and to congested birth spacing, due to the absence of reproductive health facilities in her community. The distressing experience of losing so many children led her to oppose early marriage and to become an auxiliary health worker focused on promoting birth control use. Her aim was to ensure that Haftey would have a far happier life: 'I wish her to have a better life than mine because I am a poor woman and have many problems' (interview transcript). She saw schooling as crucial to achieving this goal, as it would both delay the girl's marriage and prepare her for a good job: 'I expect her to have a better life because she will be educated and she will have a job… I sent her to school because I want her to have a better life…' (interview transcript). 'Now, there is smartness…. Of course they are smart, we are happy that our children are going to school' (interview transcript).

Rural children fall behind their urban peers

The Young Lives sample in each study country was selected randomly from 20 communities spread across a mix of urban and rural areas. Young Lives has found important differences between children living in different communities, and it is apparent that the benefits of national economic growth and development in the four countries have been unequally shared between urban and rural populations. Many Young Lives households remain vulnerable to food insecurity and to shocks – unexpected economic, environmental or family events, such as drought or death, which have adverse consequences for individuals and households. While the percentage of Young Lives households in Ethiopia reporting food insecurity in the previous year fell from 38% to 28% between 2009 and 2016, a significant proportion of the poorest households continue to face food insecurity, in that country and also in Vietnam (Benny et al, 2018). In three countries, reporting of adverse impacts of economic shocks was especially evident in 2009, and was driven largely by increased food and input prices associated with the global financial crisis (Dornan, 2010). As Figure 3.2 shows, household

Figure 3.2: Percentage of households reporting adverse impacts from economic shocks, 2016

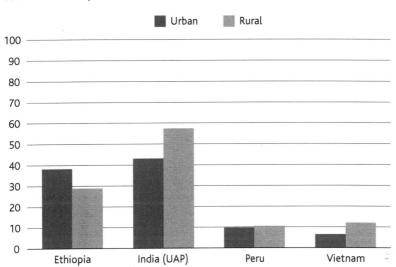

exposure to economic shocks remained high in 2016 for two countries even during periods of economic growth. Economic shocks often affect urban households more than they do rural households because urban populations cannot grow their own produce and have to purchase everything they need; the adverse impact is particularly evident in Ethiopia.

Urban communities are typically better off than rural communities and urban households enjoy better service access, housing quality and consumer durables. This is illustrated by Figures 3.3 and 3.4, which track changes in material conditions in Ethiopia and Vietnam by averaging the wealth level across the households in each community in the years 2002 and 2016 (survey rounds 1 and 5). Though all communities saw gains during this period, there were very large differences in average wealth levels between them. With only a couple of exceptions, the ranking remained constant over time. The circumstances facing children in the different communities are very dissimilar: from the nature of work, to access to services and transport and levels of exposure to extreme weather conditions such as drought or floods.

The poorest Ethiopian site is Weyn, a rural community in the Southern Nations, Nationalities and Peoples' Region in the south west of the country. Weyn is prone to serious environmental hazards, including drought. The least poor site is Menderin, a slum community

Figure 3.3: Average wealth levels in communities, 2002 and 2016: Ethiopia

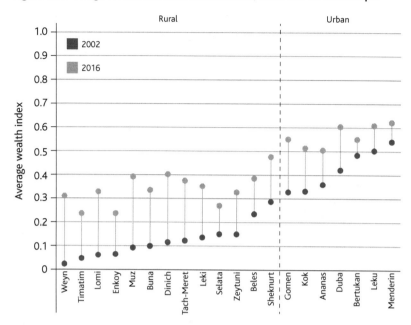

Note: The figure includes all Young Lives households (Younger and Older Cohorts) providing information at each round.

in the capital, Addis Ababa, which nevertheless faces a range of problems, such as poor physical safety and low-quality services.

The poorest Vietnamese community, Lang Hoi, is in one of the northern hilly provinces bordering China where remoteness makes transport and trading difficult. A high proportion of the population of Lang Hoi comprises minority ethnic groups that have traditionally been economically and socially disadvantaged. By contrast, the least poor site, Nhan Trung, is part of Da Nang, a large and prosperous port city that depends on trade and has good services and transport links. The apparently lower economic growth among sites with higher average wealth levels (which tended to be urban) is partly due to the nature of the wealth index which specifies the services, housing conditions and consumer durables to which the respondent may or may not have access. Hence these, urban households already had access to the majority of the items assessed by the index in the first survey round, so it was unlikely for them to experience further gains in subsequent rounds.

Figure 3.4: Average wealth levels in communities, 2002 and 2016: Vietnam

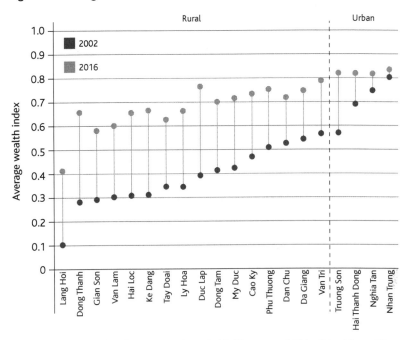

Note: The figure includes all Young Lives households (Younger and Older Cohorts) providing information at each round.

Despite rapid improvements in services across all four countries, with overall coverage in 2016 consistently higher than in 2002, service access is another aspect of life in which rural communities lag behind urban communities, as illustrated by Figure 3.5.

There are many other ways in which rural children are more disadvantaged than their urban peers. Rural populations experience more risk than urban populations, for example through more frequent exposure to extreme weather events such as drought, which can be a major cause of livelihood insecurity. Figure 3.6 shows that rural households are consistently more likely to report environmental shocks than urban ones throughout the 10 years from 2006 to 2016, even though national economies were growing during this period.

Poorer rural households are particularly susceptible to such shocks, since they often depend on rain-fed agriculture and lack the kind of technology and equipment that may help them adapt. Moreover, poor families may not be able to access loans or credit from financial institutions, or from relatives, neighbours or friends, who may be

Figure 3.5: Rural sanitation and drinking water coverage for Younger Cohort households, 2002 and 2016 (%)

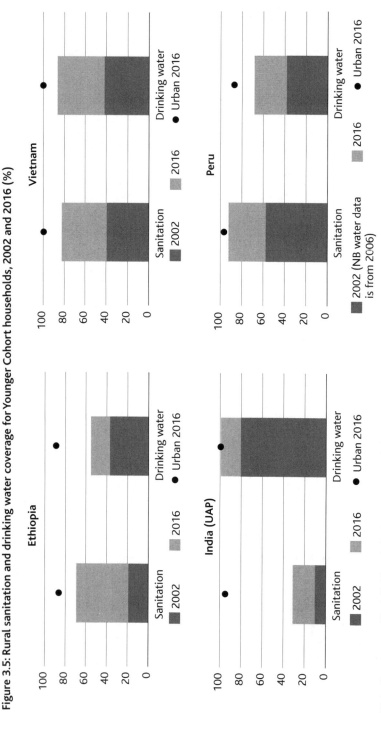

Note: Country-specific definitions in basic sanitation and clean drinking water mean that this data is not comparable across countries.

Figure 3.6: Percentage of households reporting adverse impacts from environmental shocks, 2005/06-16

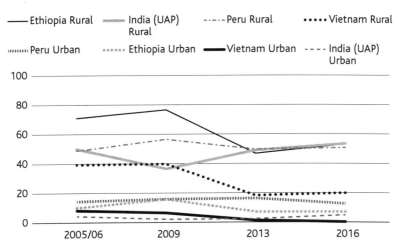

Note: The figure includes all Young Lives households (Younger and Older Cohorts) providing information at each round.

exposed to the same threats. One Young Lives mother living in a drought prone area in the Tigray region of Ethiopia described stark choices, although at least she had been able to access some government support:

> Now due to the drought we are thinking to sell the cattle to use it for our consumption and send our children to school. We are not yet sure whether we will have enough to survive from the [Productive] Safety Net [Programme] and other income activities and if the income is not enough we will borrow from the Government. (Quoted in Ogando Portela and Pells, 2015a, p 77)

In contrast, a Scheduled Tribe boy from United Andhra Pradesh described the impact of heavy rains: 'We faced some problems, they happened this year. There were floods and all the fields were inundated. Heavy rains damaged the crops and everyone's farmland was badly affected' (quoted in Young Lives, 2012, p 1). He explained that, as a consequence, 'We were forced to buy rice and other things since then from outside.... Whatever little money we earned was spent on buying rice' (quoted in Young Lives, 2012, p 12).

Children exposed to extreme weather events in early childhood are likely to be shorter than their peers and to suffer from illnesses such as diarrhoea, which affects their nutrient absorption, and may curtail growth (Georgiadis, 2016). Children may also be affected through threats to their mothers' wellbeing, health and nutrition. For example, children born to mothers who were exposed to the 1984 famine in Ethiopia were found to be shorter and behind in their schooling compared with those whose mothers were not affected (Tafere, 2016).

The urban–rural gap is also reflected in perceived life opportunities, as revealed in intentions to migrate. In rural areas throughout the four countries there is a widespread aspiration for children to move to the city, with the expectation that they will earn more, have an easier life and remit income back to their families. This dream is shared by boys, girls, mothers, fathers and grandparents alike. Eva, from a rural community in Peru, is among many Young Lives children who have resolved to move to the city. Eva helped her parents out on their farm, but found the work tiring, dirty and unpleasant. She complained that she regularly felt 'shattered' at the end of the day and declared, 'I am not going to be a peasant' (quoted in Boyden, 2013, p 8). She was determined to seek out a better life by moving to Lima, and her plan was to train to be a nurse. Schooling is often the main vehicle through which children migrate from rural areas, as rural families commonly support the transition of adolescents to urban secondary schools in the search for better quality or more prestigious education (see Chapter Six). Nicolas also lives in rural Peru. The death of his father had an enormous impact on the family. His mother was convinced that his route out of poverty meant finishing secondary school, going to university in the city and becoming a 'professional'. His two elder sisters were already living in Lima and sent money for Nicolas's education. His mother stated: '[I] always dream ... that the city isn't like here; here it's always suffering.... I tell him to "study son, it's for you, what's of the *chacra* (fields) stays *chacra*, your studies, no one can take them away"' (quoted in Crivello and Boyden, 2011, p 15).

Children in urban areas still face many risks

Although families and children living in towns and cities are generally better off than their rural counterparts, and despite the aspirations of rural populations to migrate to the city, Young Lives children and caregivers are clear that urban slum dwelling carries its own problems. Lack of safety, uncollected rubbish, poor hygiene and sanitation, and low levels of social trust are mentioned regularly. Amira and Miki are growing up in Addis Ababa, in sites with the highest wealth level in the Ethiopian sample. Even so, their home is very cramped. Miki's grandmother, his caregiver, said:

> We are living here because we do not have any other option. Our house is very small. We do all things here. We cook here, we eat here, we sleep here and all of our belongings are here. (Quoted in Pankhurst and Tiumelissan, 2013, p 17).

Amira's mother complained about having to rely on public toilets and the difficulties this presented for children:

> It is very sad to talk about our toilet. There is no toilet in the compound and near our house, so we are supposed to walk 3–5 minutes and pay 25 cents to use one. This might be tolerable for adults, but it is very difficult for children, so we are using a bedpan for them. The toilet is shared by many people. (Quoted in Pankhurst and Tiumelissan, 2013, p 12)

In Peru, Carmen expressed frustration at adults' failure to appreciate the environment:

> I would like [my locality] to be more green, and cleaner as well. People don't have awareness. They throw things over there in the gutter, thinking it's the rubbish bin. They throw stuff there. It makes me angry. Once, a lady ... I think it was orange juice, she threw the bag into the gutter. I didn't say anything, but I think that if I had complained, I would have said 'What's the matter with you? Why are you throwing that there, if that is not for rubbish?' (Quoted in Young Lives, 2012, p 8)

Also in Peru, Luz explained that the dirty and 'ugly' streets in her town, San Roman, made her feel bad (Young Lives, 2012) and Fabian complained that when the waste collection in his neighbourhood in Lima was suspended for six months the area 'looked bad'.

Lack of personal safety in urban areas due to a felt or real threat of violence and crime is a critical concern for many. Luz said:

> Well, [it's] not so good.... The noise and a bit.... Well, the thieves frighten me.... Whatever time of day, they can

come in. When you're not home, they can come inside and take everything, leaving your house practically empty. (Quoted in Young Lives, 2012, p 8)

Equally, Susan, in Lima, declared:

> I prefer to go to school in the morning, because in the afternoons it is more dangerous – when I come back it is darker. I mean it is dangerous – in the streets there is always danger – but in the morning it is not so dangerous. It is less likely that something happens to you [in the morning], but in the streets at night, there are more adult people, drunken people. I don't know, it is more dangerous. (Quoted in Pells, 2011b, p 25)

Concerns about the absence of secure tenure is also a significant worry for many. For example, residents of Bertukan in Addis Ababa face eviction and relocation as part of the government's development plans (Pankhurst and Tiumelissan, 2013). Adjacent areas have been demolished and they have been told that they too will soon have to move. Relocated families are generally rehoused, although many have found that their new accommodation is far from sources of livelihood, family and friends, and sometimes also far from key services like schools.

Some children face multiple hazards, with cumulative adverse effects

Household economic position and access to infrastructure and services are not simply a matter of where families live, but also relate closely to social status. Social inequalities are unique in each context, but minority social status, whether due to language, religious, caste or ethnic differences, tends to be linked to circumstances that undermine children's outcomes everywhere. In some of the circumstances investigated by Young Lives, there has been upwards convergence: for example, enrolment gaps between different groups tend to have narrowed as primary school access has become near-universal. Similarly, across Peru, some inequalities (such as in access to sanitation and electricity) have narrowed as these services have expanded. However, it is important to note that the focus on access can mask wide variations in quality and the outcomes achieved for children and that minority communities tend to have poorer facilities and services.

While minority ethnic children often fall behind in Vietnam, in India it is girls and young people from Scheduled Castes and Scheduled Tribes who are particularly disadvantaged. Marginalised groups are more likely to live in rural areas with greater prevalence of environmental shocks and poorer services and they are generally among the most deprived in these contexts. In rural areas of United Andhra Pradesh, access to sanitation has remained stubbornly low – just 31% of rural households have a flush toilet, septic tank or pit latrine – but access among rural Scheduled Caste and Scheduled Tribe households is lower still.

Shocks are interrelated: households experiencing poverty are more likely to report economic and environmental shocks, service shortfalls, bereavement and/or family illness, and are also more likely to have reported shocks in previous survey rounds. Illness may generate huge care demands, while the labour contribution of the person who is sick must be replaced. Kassaye's mother, in rural Ethiopia, highlighted how her family had been hit by multiple catastrophes. When her husband broke his leg, he was unable to work for six months during the sowing season, when the family's labour needs were high. The harvest also failed, so they went hungry (Pells, 2011a). Medical treatment is often extremely expensive, as is transport to and from medical facilities. The most consistent complaints about these costs came from United Andhra Pradesh. One father described the implications of several members of his family falling ill at the same time:

> In a month if anyone is affected [in this case by malaria and typhoid], it passes to all the others in the family. When the first one is being treated with medical care and everything and he is almost back to normal, another child becomes affected by the same disease, and then my wife, it is like that. The money we got as income is all spent on medical care. (Quoted in Pells, 2011a, p 20)

Similarly, Ravi, who is from a Scheduled Caste and lives in a rural community, explained that his mother suffered from stomach pains, headaches and the chikungunya virus. She consulted private doctors, believing them to be more conscientious, so his family had to take out loans to pay the medical bills, the debt reaching a full 28,000 rupees. Repayment was dependent on a good harvest and Ravi's work in a local town (Pells, 2011a). Govindh's mother also fell ill and her medical costs reached 10,000 rupees. The harvest failed two years running and Govindh's family was only able to cope by borrowing money from his uncle and his grandmother's village (Pells and Woodhead, 2014).

Not all change is perceived as improving children's wellbeing

In a time of dramatic economic and socio-cultural change, there may be significant transformations also in social norms and values, leading sometimes to considerable anxiety and even conflict within families over how best to raise children. In Vietnam, caregivers expressed concerns about the influence of modern attitudes and practices on the young, particularly the potential of their being 'corrupted' by 'social evils' such as pornography, drugs, early sexual activity, divorce, family breakdown and alcoholism (Zharkevich et al, 2016, p 9). While there are obvious benefits, it is striking that for caregivers – in Vietnam particularly – digital technology, especially mobile telephones and the internet, is one of the most worrying aspects of modern life. The internet was sometimes described as a 'vice'. One mother in Da Nang said: '… the Internet … has become prevalent in the last three or four years.… The consequences of the Internet are very serious. At school, students often fight with teachers' (interview transcript). Another mother suggested that the influence of the internet is undermining parents' abilities to control their children: 'We can't control the children. Sometimes we are too busy doing businesses and can't follow them all the time. Although I know this, I can't do anything to prevent them' (interview transcript). Another said:

> Around here there are a lot of social problems/evils. In many cases, students drop out [of] lessons at the school to play games online in the Internet cafes nearby the school. Like in Viet – Korea school, every time I go to workplace I see during class time, but there are still many students, sitting in the Internet café playing games. So I am afraid that my son will be in the same situation. (Interview transcript)

Some caregivers fear that their children are not being taught basic skills properly due to the use of the Internet in schools. In Lima, Peru, Alejandro's mother said:

> Now there aren't good teachers … because now everything is Internet. Before there were better teachers.… The teachers that used to teach us before, made us do homework that we had to do *with our own hands*. (Interview transcript; emphasis added)

Caregivers have concerns about other aspects of modern life that they perceive to be increasingly outside their control. Latha's brother eloped with a girl and her mother was worried about Latha having too much freedom, with the risk that this would undermine the family's reputation: 'If she studies here and there, goes to towns, friendships are formed [with boys]. That may happen. So, we stopped' (quoted in Pells, 2011b, p 8). At age 15, Latha was no longer enrolled in school, but instead working in the fields, and being taught domestic skills in readiness for marriage. Latha did have a say in her marriage and although involving young people in such important decisions may be seen as a positive development, her mother expressed a concern that nowadays young people take little account of their elders: 'If we tell them one thing, they do the other thing. Now it is not like our days, they don't listen to elders. They say "We cannot live the same way as you"' (interview transcript).

Some of the recent changes in norms in relation to the young have arisen through government policies aimed at changing child-rearing practice to better protect children. On occasion, efforts to bring about social change through policy and legal measures have had unintended adverse consequences. This highlights the importance of understanding the logic underlying social values and practices. For example, the Ethiopian government has taken a strong stand against early marriage and female genital mutilation/cutting (FGM/C), and imposes fines and imprisonment for infractions. Many Young Lives caregivers recognise the advantages for girls of staying in school longer and marrying later, and many understand that FGM/C poses potential health risks. But raising the legal age of marriage and banning FGM/C have caused considerable apprehension and intra-familial conflict. Ethiopia is a patriarchal society and many believe that FGM/C ensures a girl's marriageability by enhancing her femininity (Boyden, 2012). Marriage, in turn, is considered to protect girls from social and economic risks in a context of poverty and vulnerability (Pankhurst, 2014). Thus, many view both FGM/C and early marriage as a necessary part of a girl's transition to adulthood.

Caregivers perceive promiscuity, elopements among teenagers and abductions of girls to have risen sharply as a consequence of delaying marriage, and associate these practices with an increase in rape, illegitimacy, unsafe abortions, abandonment of women and their offspring, and higher rates of sexually transmitted infections in the young. All of their concerns are intensified by the lack of reproductive health facilities and limited support for young unmarried mothers with children. When FGM/C was banned, caregivers often felt it imperative to comply with the law. But some girls sought to conduct their own secret operations, wishing to ensure they would be marriageable, and these procedures were often more dangerous due to their clandestine nature. Adults expressed deep concern about girls organising their own circumcisions. A father from Oromia explained:

> Girls are conducting not only illegal circumcision, but they are also violating the traditional norms by carrying out circumcision at any time and under any circumstance. Most of the time circumcision [today] is conducted during the night time. This kind of secret practice is totally dangerous for the life of the girls. (Quoted in Boyden, 2012, p 1118)

It is perhaps unsurprising that rapid social change can be a cause of disquiet and contestation among parents and young people regarding the best way to secure a safe transition to adulthood. In some cases, young people resisting decisions made by adults can cause them significant social and physical risk. The concerns coexist, though, with great optimism for the generational changes that more schooling will produce. This is not to suggest that such perceptions are necessarily realities, nor that the past was less risky. The presence of preventable deaths from early marriage and childbirth suggest it was not. But what this does indicate is that change can be unsettling, and that policy-makers and law makers have a responsibility to understand the social, economic and other forces sustaining particular practices. Understanding such factors is part of expanding effective policies while minimising the harm that such policies sometimes unintentionally cause.

Conclusion

During the first two decades of the millennium, most Young Lives children and their families experienced significant changes in their living circumstances. The bioecological life course model introduced in Chapter Two set out how society and policy changes frames children's development; this chapter has discussed some of the channels through which this happens. There have been many positive developments, as poverty levels and stunting rates have declined, and infrastructure and service access improved. Intergenerational progress has also been observed, with many children experiencing better health and more education than the previous generation. Gender inequalities in access to education have decreased and more young women are able to delay marriage and parenthood. And new technologies have brought many benefits, expanding children's horizons.

However, significant social and economic disparities persist, and children in rural areas and from minority groups continue to face disadvantages across many aspects of their lives. Similarly, social and economic change has not always been comfortable for all. Urban living offers many advantages, but children's wellbeing is not automatically improved. Migration to urban areas may pose new risks for children, exposing them to violence and loss of social trust. Many adults worry that new influences, such as the internet and policy interventions, may threaten the safety of children. Such concerns are understandable and indicate how parents can feel disempowered by change. The evidence also highlights the policy challenge of how best to bring an end to practices that may be harmful to children without also causing resistance and social disruption. Careful attention needs to be paid to how communities view practices considered damaging by policy-makers. Young Lives evidence highlights the importance of engaging with communities as part of the change process, and suggests that the law alone is unlikely to shift practices that are deeply rooted and may be reproduced by poverty and economic risk.

Note
[1] Data for fathers were not always collected and so these are restricted to mothers and daughters.

FOUR

Early childhood:
The essential foundation

There is now a broad consensus in research and policy that early childhood is important in laying the foundation for later development, and that growing up in poverty generally has a deleterious and long-term impact on children's wellbeing and development. While poverty occurs in all societies to a greater or lesser degree, children in LMICs are particularly affected, commonly experiencing under-nutrition, resource shortfalls and limited services supporting healthy growth and development. Poor children are also the least likely to access quality early childhood care and education (ECCE). Together, these disadvantages prevent millions of young people from realising their developmental potential (Grantham-McGregor et al, 2007; Walker et al, 2011).

Improving survival and extending access to services in this critical phase of life were key priorities championed by the Millennium Development Goals (MDGs) and child survival improved during the first 15 years of the millennium when these goals were being implemented. Even so, infant and child under-nutrition and poor health remain a central concern in many low- and middle-income countries (LMICs), as acknowledged in the current Sustainable Development Goals (SDGs). Specifically, SDG target 4.2 provides that by 2030 all girls and boys should have access to 'quality early childhood development, care and pre-primary education so that they are ready for primary education' (UNICEF, nd). The provision of quality early childhood services is now firmly on the policy agenda, though in many cases this involves a far more comprehensive approach than simply facilitating school readiness, as called for in target 4.1 (see Woodhead, 2016).

Despite the policy attention to early childhood, many poor children continue to experience environments and circumstances that undermine subsequent development, setting up disadvantages from early in life. And despite their foundational contribution to later stages of education and development, early childhood services remain under-developed in many countries. This chapter therefore focuses on what is known from Young Lives about the significance of early life, and the mechanisms by which early disadvantages shape the developmental cascade from the beginning of life. The chapter emphasises the absolute importance of a good start in early childhood as the foundation for later human development. It then discusses in detail two core development concerns: under-nutrition, and preschool circumstances and interventions. This analysis is developed further in Chapter Seven.

A healthy start has long-term benefits

Young Lives is not a study dedicated to health alone, and as a result does not have comprehensive data on children's health over the course of their development. Similarly, since families were first visited when members of the Younger Cohort were aged between 6 and 18 months, circumstances around birth are not known. This means that children were sampled after the most vulnerable first few months of life, and as such, fewer instances of infant mortality were observed. However, child growth was measured from the first year of life (Younger Cohort) and at each subsequent survey round in all four countries. This longitudinal multi-country and multifaceted approach to changing patterns of child growth is unique in cohort studies and is the focus of this section.

Early under-nutrition is a risk factor for mortality and morbidity and there is mounting evidence of the damage done to brain development, shown through impacts on cognitive development. Young Lives tracks several growth indicators, including wasting and underweight, that result from short-run under-nutrition.[1] However, the focus here is on stunting or being much shorter than expected for age, compared with the World Health Organization (WHO) growth norm standards.[2] Stunting is an indicator of chronic ill-health, under-nutrition and inadequate care, and is likely to result from a combination of factors, including a lack of food quality and quantity, the impact of poor maternal mental wellbeing, and diseases that undermine nutritional intake.

Long-term deficiencies may be due to a mix of household and caregiver determinants, such as poverty, livelihood insecurity or low maternal education, alongside community-wide factors, chiefly poor-quality sanitation, hygiene and water, and high food prices. Having young children in the household may also be a factor that contributes to food insecurity, since these children cannot contribute labour to the household or provide for themselves (Morrow et al, 2017). Families often adopt strategies to ensure that their children are fed during times of food insecurity that can, in turn, have unintended adverse effects on nutrition. These include buying cheap foods that are often low-quality, limiting their intake of fruits and vegetables, restricting portion sizes, and diluting food such as dal with water. At times adults choose not to eat in order to feed their children, as Triveni, aged 15 years, from Katur in United Andhra Pradesh noted: 'Mother provides food for the children by fasting herself' (quoted in Aurino and Morrow, 2018, p 219). Even so, child stunting still occurs. Stunting in early childhood often sets up a pattern that persists throughout life, and through its association with impaired cognition and delayed school progression is a key early channel by which poverty in childhood results in lost human potential.

Figures 4.1 and 4.2 give insight into the likelihood of persistence in stunting through childhood and adolescence by depicting average patterns of growth up to age 15. Figure 4.1 indicates the rates of stunting among the Younger Cohort between ages 1 and 15 in all countries. It shows how common stunting was within the Young Lives sample at the outset of the study and also that average levels have subsequently changed.

In three of the countries, stunting rates rose between ages 1 and 5 years, and then in all four countries they subsequently gradually fell. This pattern is common in low-income countries (De Onis and Branca, 2016) and is frequently a consequence of a combination of poor nutrition after cessation of breast feeding, and diarrhoea and other diseases associated with poor sanitation and water conditions. Such evidence was crucial to the identification of the first 1,000 days of life from conception as a critical intervention point. Directing attention to the first 1,000 days is an important step, since it is an optimal period in the life course for intervening with children, as well as mothers, whose health is also vital to a good start in life. Young Lives evidence found Ethiopia to be an exception to the trend, with initial stunting rates much higher and an increase at age 5 far less apparent than in the other countries.

Stunting rates have reduced over time as a result of policies and societal development

Improvements in children's circumstances in all four study countries can be seen by comparing the height of the two Young Lives cohorts at the same ages. Comparisons are possible at ages 8, 12 and 15 (inter-cohort comparison of stunting rates in early childhood is not possible, since this information is not available for the Older Cohort). Height at age 8 is likely to be indicative of earlier circumstances. A reduction in stunting at age 8 between the cohorts was evident in all

Figure 4.1: Younger Cohort stunting rates by country and age (1-15 years)

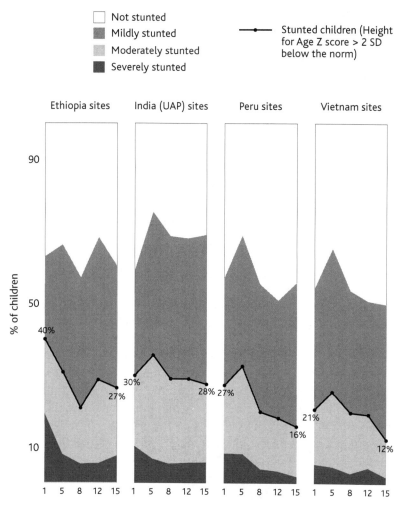

Note: Each column stacks up to 100% of surveyed children. Shaded areas demonstrate the severity of stunting at age points between 1 and 15 years. 'Severely stunted' is measured three or more standard deviations below the WHO reference norm, 'moderately stunted' between two and three standard deviations below the norm, 'mildly stunted' between 0 and one standard deviation below the norm.

four countries, this being particularly dramatic in Peru (from 33% for the Older Cohort to 22% for the Younger Cohort; Cueto et al, 2011), and smallest in United Andhra Pradesh (from 33% to 29%; Galab et al, 2011). These figures indicate improvements for children growing up in the same communities. The rapid reduction in child stunting in Peru has been linked to policy efforts, including dedicated nutrition interventions and the *Juntos* conditional cash transfer programme (see also WHO, 2014b).

The poorest children are the most likely to be stunted

Within these average reductions, however, are wide socioeconomic differences, with the poorest children, children in rural rather than urban areas, those with less educated mothers, and those from minority ethnic backgrounds typically having the highest stunting rates. Figure 4.2 shows that differences in wealth levels also set children on radically different growth trajectories and that gaps related to wealth levels persist through the early life course. The figure uses data from United Andhra Pradesh, where the poorest third of children were roughly twice as likely to be stunted as the least poor third. This pattern, namely that the poorest children are most likely to be stunted, is common across the countries.

Figure 4.2: Stunting rates for the poorest and least poor children, India (UAP)

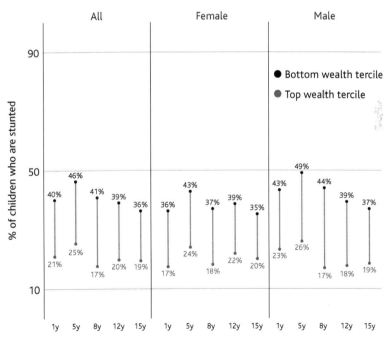

Source: Data for this visualisation is taken from all rounds of the Young Lives survey. The data includes younger cohort individuals for whom there is information in all rounds of the survey

Figure 4.2 shows who is affected by growth deficiencies, but not why. Poverty, location, service access, education levels and ethnicity are all often closely related. Figure 4.3 again highlights the different growth trajectories of the Younger Cohort children, this time distinguishing those living in rural areas from their urban counterparts. It shows that the former are far more likely to be stunted than the latter in all countries and at all ages, even though average stunting rates declined with age. The rural–urban disparity is most pronounced in Peru, a country with high levels of inequality where children in rural areas have a much higher risk of being stunted than children in urban areas, but this disparity is not nearly as high in Peru.

Much of the urban–rural disparity lies in differences in wealth and service levels and material circumstances (Nolan, 2016). The evidence from Peru reinforces this point. While children in rural areas were much more likely to be stunted overall than those in urban areas, children in the poorest quintile in urban areas were four times more likely to be stunted than those in the wealthiest quintile (Woodhead et al, 2013a). Location matters, but it is what happens to children and households in different places that matters most. Children from wealthier households were not only the least likely to be stunted, but also the most likely to recover from early childhood stunting. This finding may indicate that better-off families are better able to make compensatory investments. It should also be noted that the Young Lives wealth measure includes access to services, which are not just vital for early growth but can be a

Figure 4.3: Rural–urban stunting rates among the Younger Cohort

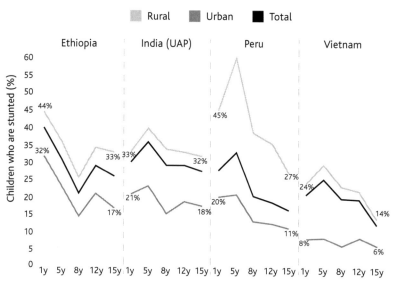

key driver of growth recovery, as has been suggested for Ethiopia (Outes-Leon and Porter, 2013). Growth recovery is discussed in Chapter Five.

Boys are typically more likely to be stunted than girls, which points to boys being more vulnerable to health insults than girls (Wamani et al, 2007). Maintaining height-for-age through childhood has also been linked to mothers' heights (Dornan and Georgiadis, 2015; Benny et al, 2017). Taller mothers tend to have taller children, and stunted mothers are more likely to have stunted children. Such links are most likely to operate both through genetics and through mothers' health prior to and/or during conception, which affects children's health (Plomin, 2018). Being born to a younger stunted mother, for example, increased the chances of children being stunted by 15 percentage points in the Young Lives data, and most of this effect was due to the mothers' stunting (Benny et al, 2017). Differences are particularly evident in Peru where stunting is higher among children from groups whose maternal tongue is indigenous, these groups being more likely than Spanish speakers to be poor and to live in rural areas. That parental education levels are associated with stunting levels also indicates that parents with less education may be poorer and live in more rural areas. Higher education levels may also suggest greater social capital, knowledge and access to support services that help children's nutrition. There are complications in interpreting the evidence, though. While the WHO standards reflect some ethnic diversity in their growth norms, not all ethnicities are represented and there is some discussion, for example, as to whether indigenous people in Peru are inherently shorter than those of European extraction (Benny et al, 2018).

At the meso and macro levels, there is a set of environmental factors around the child that can compromise early development (Bronfenbrenner and Morris, 2006): from sanitation and its safe use (which reduces the incidence of infectious disease), to the quality of the natural environment (including risks such as drought and food insecurity). As noted, some of these are reflected in our definition of household wealth and so greater wealth is likely to be predictive of important protective factors such as food security and so is frequently found to be linked with lower risk of stunting (see Benny et al, 2018).

Stunting is linked to substantial lost development potential

In recent decades, there has been an increasing awareness of the links between physical growth and children's cognitive capacity (reviewed by Prendergast and Humphrey, 2014). Two mechanisms are likely to underpin this link. First, conditions such as inadequate nutrition or childhood infectious disease that contribute to early stunting undermine areas of the brain associated with cognitive functioning. Second, the consequences of stunting, from poor child health to later school achievement, bode poorly for cognitive abilities. The question of how the child's growth is associated with other aspects of development has been widely studied within Young Lives (see, for example, Aurino and Burchi, 2014; Dornan and Georgiadis, 2015; Georgiadis and Penny, 2017; Benny et al, 2018). Evidence exists across early childhood, middle childhood and adolescence that not being stunted and having greater height-for-age is associated with higher subsequent performance in tests of language and mathematics abilities.

One Young Lives study considered the relationship between low height-for-age in infancy, and receptive vocabulary at age 5 years (Sánchez, 2009). Having controlled for background characteristics, an increase of one standard deviation[3] of height-for-age at age 1 corresponded to a rise of between 4% (Ethiopia) and 12% (India UAP) of a standard deviation in receptive vocabulary test scores. These effect sizes were found to be smaller than those associated with a similar sized increase in maternal education and household per capita consumption, but larger than those associated with improvements in basic services (Sánchez, 2009). Using a range of different quantitative techniques, studies again suggest significant medium- and long-term damage to children's cognitive development associated with early under-nutrition (for example, Woldehanna et al, 2017). Similar results can also be seen at older ages with an increase in earlier height-for-age being associated with an increase in cognitive skills (see Sánchez, 2017). As well as stunting being linked to low levels of numeracy and vocabulary development, there is evidence that low height-for-age is also associated with low self-efficacy and other psycho-social attributes (Dercon and Sánchez, 2013).

We return to the discussion of children's height growth, and its relation with cognitive development during middle childhood, in Chapters Five and Seven.

Early learning programmes enhance literacy and numeracy

Programmes that relate specifically to health and survival (such as vaccination or breast feeding) are now relatively well established and have achieved significant reductions in child mortality and under-nutrition. Nevertheless, service quality and delivery remain major challenges in low-income countries (UNESCO, 2015). Recognising the importance of early learning in child development and preparation for school, UNESCO Education For All Goal 1 called for expanded and improved 'early childhood care and education, especially for the most vulnerable and disadvantaged children' (UNESCO, 2006, p 6), while, as noted, a key target of SDG 4 is to ensure both access and quality early childhood care and education (ECCE). Using data from the Younger Cohort, findings reported here address access and then outcomes for children who attended preschool.

Though 'quality' is given prominence in SDG 4, there is a lack of clarity in what this actually means in the ECCE programme context. Variable country resources and differing cultural values are placed on children developing particular attributes and skills, and the definition and measurement of quality indicators for ECCE is complex and contested (Woodhead, 1996; Myers, 2001, 2006). Most research on predictors of learning outcomes has been conducted in centre-based programmes. Early learning programmes, which include preschool services such as kindergarten, have received considerable attention since the Dakar Declaration of the World Education Forum in 2000 (UNESCO, 2000). Common indicators focus on inputs such as the physical setting, teacher–child ratio, group size, teacher qualifications and learning materials; process variables that predict better learning outcomes include a balance of free-choice activities with carefully selected materials, and interactions with qualified teachers that scaffold learning. The literature indicates that at least 15 to 20 hours of programme exposure per week is required to improve learning outcomes (UNICEF, 2008).

The poorest children have worse receptive vocabulary than other groups by age 5

Table 4.1 shows that gaps in learning levels were evident the first time the children were tested, at age 5 on receptive vocabulary (see Appendix 1 for an explanation of the measure used to test receptive vocabulary). The differences between boys and girls were small, but

Table 4.1: Receptive vocabulary gaps, age 5

	Ethiopia	India (UAP)	Peru	Vietnam
Boys–girls	1.0%	0.5%	0.8%	0.8%
Top quintile–bottom quintile of wealth index in round 1	7.8%	8.8%	23.0%	12.2%
Maternal education	5.8%	8.5%	14.3%	7.6%

Note: Differences reported are percentage point differences between the average % of correct answers.

Source: Cueto et al (2016)

as a function of socioeconomic status (both wealth and maternal education), they were much larger.

These skills are an important indicator for school readiness, and therefore affect the likelihood of children progressing well within the early grades of school.

The poorest children often missed out on preschool

Data on preschool enrolment in the Younger Cohort were collected from the child's caregiver at round 2 of the survey (2006) for all countries except Ethiopia (where they were collected in 2009, at round 3). Respondents were asked whether the child had attended a preschool or childcare facility/crèche at any time since the age of 3, and for how long (for example, six months or a year). Under this criterion, most of the children would have been eligible in the years 2003-05. National programme types were specified, as well as whether they were provided by the state, a private business, a non-governmental organisation (NGO) or a faith-based institution. Depending on the country, types of provision varied from formal centre-based preschools through home-visiting programmes and other forms of community-based provision. Participation by country is shown in Table 4.2.

Differences are evident across the national samples. In Ethiopia, three quarters of Young Lives children had no preschool exposure, while participation rates were greater than 80% in Peru, United Andhra Pradesh and Vietnam. In the period since Young Lives children were at preschool age Ethiopia has been making significant efforts to extend provision, particularly through 'O' Class public kindergartens for six-year-olds (Woodhead et al, 2017). In Vietnam provision is largely the responsibility of the state, and since the country makes significant investment nationally in education, the high participation rate is

Table 4.2: Younger Cohort: early learning programme enrolment (number, %)

	Type of provision 2003-05			
	Never participated	Private	Public	Community/ other
Ethiopia	1,436 (75%)	337 (18%)	60 (3%)	78 (4%)
India (UAP)	255 (12%)	523 (27%)	1,167 (60%)	5 (0.26%)
Peru	208 (11%)	212 (11%)	1,203 (62%)	315 (16%)
Vietnam	184 (9%)	184 (9%)	1,540 (78%)	59 (3%)

Note: All percentages have been rounded up.

Source: Favara et al (forthcoming)

perhaps a consequence. Unsurprisingly, wealthier children are more likely to participate in the private system in all four countries, and wealthier urban and ethnic majority children have higher participation rates overall (Murray and Woodhead, 2010).

Figure 4.4 shows the relationship between household wealth (in this case measured by monthly expenditure) and preschool participation for the Younger Cohort in two very different countries, Ethiopia and Peru. When the children were at preschool age, the two countries had

Figure 4.4: Preschool participation in two Young Lives samples by household expenditure

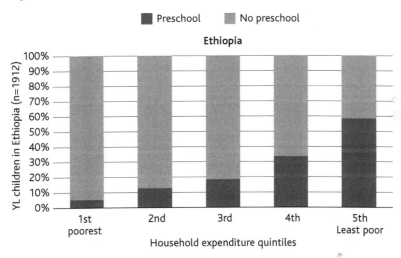

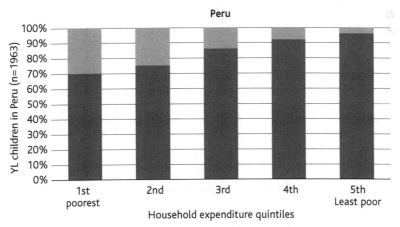

Note: It is assumed that children would have attended before or during or the year after the round 2 survey (when children were 5 years old). The prescribed age of grade 1 enrolment is 7 years in Ethiopia and 6 years in Peru.

Source: Woodhead et al (2009)

very different levels of resource and policy regimes. Peru, a middle-income country, had significant public provision, and Ethiopia, a low-income country, had minimal state-financed early childhood education. While in both countries participation among the poor was lower than among other groups, comparison between them reveals stark differences. Whereas 70% of the poorest children in Peru accessed a preschool programme of some kind, in Ethiopia, the figure for the poorest quintile was less than 10%.

Nevertheless, despite Peru's policy of publicly funded access for poor and rural children, inequalities in access persist. Young Lives qualitative data provide an informative example. In 2007, Carmen was 5 years old and lived with her parents and teenage sister in a rural village in the Peruvian high *selva* (jungle). Although the early learning centre was only 15 minutes' walk from her home, and Carmen expressed a desire to go, her parents decided not to send her. The walk to the centre was dangerous, along a busy main highway, and no one in the family could accompany Carmen in the mornings because of school and work commitments. When primary school began in 2008, Carmen was able to attend because other children in the neighbourhood walked with her. Carmen's challenges with accessing early childhood education highlight that programmes that wish to include all children need to adapt to local families' needs, for example by making hours of classes more flexible (Streuli, 2012).

In addition to poverty and rurality affecting preschool access, inequities in access on ethnic grounds were evident in all the countries. For example, in Peru, 90% of the Spanish-speaking sample had access, compared with just 45% of Quechua- or Aymara-speaking children (Escobal et al, 2008).

Preschool has positive impacts on children's development

It is important to understand whether and in what ways children who attend early learning programmes benefit from the experience. The answer from several analyses of Young Lives data is clearly that they do. Across the Young Lives countries, the opportunity to participate in a preschool programme is shown to have benefits for language development. In Ethiopia, better-off urban children who attended mainly private preschool education scored significantly higher on a measure of receptive vocabulary (described in Appendix 1) at 5 years than those who did not participate, after controlling for household wealth (Woldehanna, 2011). Associations have also been found between preschool attendance and attainment, on-time school enrolment and grade progression through middle childhood (Vandemoortele, 2018). In the long term, those who participated in preschool were close to 26% more likely to have completed secondary schooling, with the rates higher for those with two or three years of preschool as against one year (Woldehanna et al, 2017).

Young Lives did not directly collect data on early learning programme attendance or programme quality, although the importance of 'quality' has been considered in many publications (for example, Rossiter, 2016). All four countries have some form of community-based early learning programmes supported by NGOs and in some instances by government, as well as both publicly funded and private centre-based programmes. These categories have been used in the research as proxies for probable variation in quality (see also Chapter Seven).

School quality emerged as a consistent theme in interviews with parents. Findings across Peru, Ethiopia and United Andhra Pradesh revealed specific challenges with preschool education in rural areas. Rural government programmes were often seen as being of lower quality, and parents complained of a lack of learning materials, large class sizes, untrained teachers and poor infrastructure, including leaking roofs and lack of chairs (Streuli et al, 2011). There are parallels to be drawn across the study countries regarding the low pay and training of early education centre staff, who are often women from poor rural areas, working with few resources (Murray and Woodhead, 2010). According to a primary school teacher in Ethiopia:

> The government has not given emphasis to pre-school education in the rural areas. Although the expectation of the government was that private and non-governmental organisations would be involved in the expansion of kindergarten both in the urban and rural areas, this has not worked in the rural areas. (Quoted in Woodhead et al, 2009, p 19)

It was reported that there were often between 40 to 50 children per teacher in Ethiopian preschools, and teachers across Ethiopia and Peru agreed that the government did not provide any materials, such as books or paint (Murray and Woodhead, 2010). In United Andhra Pradesh, fieldwork in 2007 confirmed a lack of play and learning materials in early education centres, whether because there were none, or they were kept locked away by teachers who considered them too valuable for use by children (Streuli et al, 2011).

Even though parents are aware of these constraints, they still send their children to the preschools when they can. As the mother of Revaneth in United Andhra Pradesh shared:

> [The school] is not at all good. In our village the teachers are not good. We just send them so that they get used to the routine of going to school…. The teachers here are not teaching well. (Quoted in Woodhead, 2009, p 16)

The mother of Shanmukha Priya, a girl in rural Poompuhar, United Andhra Pradesh, explained that parents send their children to low-quality schools because there are no alternatives if a family cannot afford tuition fees at private schools (Streuli et al, 2011).

Violence at preschools also emerged as a concern across several contexts. For example, in Ethiopia, the report of a young boy, Addisu, who had been to a private preschool was said to be typical:

> Even though I was very happy with the education, sometimes the teachers beat us even when we hadn't been naughty. There is one old woman in the school. She looks out for us when we are late and hits us with a strong stick. She also beat us when we didn't wash our hands after having food. I was afraid of her. I hate to get hit. (Quoted in Woodhead et al, 2013a, p 24)

And in Peru, the account by Hugo's mother (when Hugo was 5 and attending a government preschool) raises safety concerns even for very young children:

> He started pre-school at the age of 4 years but dropped out only five months later, after an incident during which another child threw a stone at him. Hugo needed stitches to the wound on his head, and from that moment he refused to go back to pre-school. According to his mother he used to say: 'I'm not going; no, I'm not going. Do you want me to get killed? Do you want them to hit me?' 'Do you want them … to crack my head open?' (Quoted in Woodhead et al, 2009, p 43)

The Peru example may be an unusual one, but perhaps it highlights a more general problem, that safety concerns are a barrier to participation.

There are some important indirect findings that suggest quality affects later outcomes. In United Andhra Pradesh, 5-year-olds who attended private preschools achieved higher mathematics scores at age 12 than those who attended publicly provisioned preschool or had no preschool exposure (although there was no advantage for vocabulary development). Furthermore, those who enrolled before age 4 showed long-term beneficial effects of attendance on both literacy and mathematics, even after taking account of differences in the household backgrounds of those who enrolled before 4 (Singh and Mukherjee, 2017). An implication for policy, consistent with these findings, is therefore that two years' attendance prior to school is better than one year. Diaz (2006) examined the effects of the type of ELP on children's performance in tests of language and numeracy in Peru. Children who attended formal, centre-based, programmes performed better than those who attended a publicly funded PRONOEI (*Programas no Escolarizados de Educación Inicial*) intended for poor rural and urban children, while there was no difference between the performance of the latter children and those who had no ELP exposure. The variable influence of the different programmes was evident at age 5 and persisted until age 8 and beyond (Diaz, 2006; Cueto et al, 2015; Favara et al, forthcoming).[4]

High-quality preschool provision gives children a boost in life since those who perform well in early grades tend to continue to stay ahead (Duncan et al, 2007; Siegler et al, 2012). This is apparent from an analysis of the relationship between preschool exposure in the Younger Cohort and mathematics scores in later years (Favara et al, forthcoming). There is considerable variation across the countries. The effect of preschool on mathematics skills at 8 and 12 years is most evident in Ethiopia. In that country, as well as in Peru and United Andhra Pradesh, those who received private preschool education (probably of better quality) performed best. In Vietnam, preschool provision is provided by the state (although private provision is available), and as we have seen, participation is almost universal among Young Lives children. By age 8, there is no association between preschool attendance and numeracy skills in Vietnam (Favara et al, forthcoming). Overall, the Vietnamese children outperform their peers in the other countries. We surmise that this is likely due to a combination of both better publicly funded preschools and primary schools, as well as parental investment in their children's education.

In general, Young Lives data show that participation in preschool enhances children's performance in tests of language and mathematics through middle childhood. Private preschool attendance further advantages young children in both areas of cognitive development. While we cannot be sure given the lack of preschool quality assessments in Young Lives, this is likely to be a function of better-quality provision for the better-off (Woodhead et al, 2009). Indications are that, apart from Vietnam, publicly funded preschools are of limited to poor quality and children who attend these do not necessarily do better than children who do not participate at all. That finding ought not to be an inherent argument against public provision (which has greater reach), but rather one for better quality.

Young Lives studies support the conclusion that while preschool access does have positive effects, at least through the primary school years, without scaling up quality access is not likely to produce significant advantages for children during their later school years and beyond. There is much focus currently on getting children ready for school. It is also vital that schools be ready for children, yet this seldom happens. Access without quality undermines the promise of early learning programmes, dashing the hopes of parents and stalling long-term poverty reduction efforts by policy-makers. As Woodhead and colleagues (2017, p 7) note:

> The risk to children if governments push ahead to implement early learning programmes in low-resource contexts is that millions may be enrolled in low quality pre-primary and then progress to low quality primary classrooms, and despite considerable investment, the long-term policy objective of improved human capital development is not realised.

Readiness for learning in school, in consequence, needs to begin well before formal school-joining ages. Young Lives evidence has shown that already by that point the poorest children are frequently doing least well in learning tests (see Dornan and Woodhead, 2015). The early foundation, good or bad, can then be magnified by what happens in school, as is considered in the next chapter.

Key findings of what mattered in early childhood from Young Lives

Young Lives reinforces and extends understandings of the vital importance of early life. Early childhood circumstances have long-term consequences for later development. To summarise findings so far:

- Under-nutrition, often manifested in child stunting, is a key indicator of children's development. Stunting rates have improved both across the life course and between the cohorts, and Chapter Three showed that adult height has also increased between generations. Falling stunting rates can plausibly be linked to policy intervention.
- Nevertheless, stunting remains common. Poor children, those living in rural areas, those from minority groups and those with less educated parents are the most likely to be stunted. Child stunting is closely linked to substantial lost development potential, most notably by compromising cognitive development, as well as psychosocial wellbeing. Child stunting is therefore a key channel through which poverty in childhood undermines later opportunities, with compounding affects, pushing children into a negative developmental cascade.
- Preschool access is growing. The poorest Young Lives children were the least likely to attend preschool and the least likely to be prepared for school. Young Lives children who attended preschool generally benefitted in later cognitive development in primary school. Preschool attendance therefore leads to better school readiness. Quality preschool provision (for example, formal centre-based interventions with low teacher–child ratios) is linked with the greatest later gains.

Policy interventions in early childhood

This section considers what is known about policy interventions with proven success in the early years and draws on a wider evidence base than from the Young Lives countries, using findings from policy studies and systematic reviews from LMICs. The evidence touches on three areas: nutrition and health; early learning; and support for caregivers. The first two of these areas are covered in the Young Lives evidence above. The third, support for caregivers, is included because the earlier analysis demonstrates the twin importance of maternal education and maternal health, and because the findings presented in Chapter Seven also indicate the importance of maternal mental health.

Interventions to improve nutrition and growth

Early childhood interventions are those involving the very early 'first 1,000 days' of life, and the period before children start school. Such interventions tend to focus on health (including vaccination and nutrition) and care (including language development and early learning, stimulation and school readiness). There is established evidence from LMICs that organised, quality early child development interventions can make a difference to children's long-term development. Reaching the poorest children is key to successful interventions.

Nutrition supplementation. Supplementary feeding includes meals or drinks aimed to increase nutritional intake (in preschool, a feeding station or home environment). Findings from one systematic review following supplementation identified gains in child weight and height, though noted gains were small. The greatest effects were for children under 2 years of age and for children from poorer backgrounds. The impact of supplementation given in preschool or other supervised spaces was found to result in a greater gain for children than did rations consumed at home. The authors describe the impact on cognition as 'sparse and mixed' (Kristjansson et al, 2016, p 30). A second systematic review considered both supplementation and nutrition education, identifying that both could be (independently) linked with improved children's growth, and reduced respiratory illness, but not diarrhoea (Lassi et al, 2013). A third review on supplementation for children under 5 finds negligible effects on children's growth, but warns it was based on only a small number of studies, and that there was a substantial difference in the findings across studies (Sguassero et al, 2012). Taken together, there is suggestive evidence that feeding programmes and related nutritional education programmes can have positive consequences for several aspects of children's healthy growth. Feeding programmes seem most effective for poorer children, for younger children, and in supervised spaces.

Supplementation and integrating interventions. Grantham-McGregor and colleagues (2014) examine the contribution of both nutritional supplementation (such as zinc) and child development interventions for young children (at preschools, through parents' groups, or home visiting). Their review is reliant on a small number of studies, but they combined nutritional and child development elements. The review concluded that nutritional interventions could improve growth, and that interventions such as preschool programmes, parent education groups and home visits could improve child development, and are themselves likely to be important for improving school readiness (by enhancing vocabulary skills, behaviour and so on). Notably, there was little evidence of synergistic results between the domains. A clearer story emerges of strong effects of trials, rather than programmes implemented at scale, reinforcing the importance of maintaining fidelity and quality when expanding interventions.

Vaccinations. The case for vaccination is clear; it is an important foundation of child health. However, many of the most disadvantaged children continue to miss out on common vaccination programmes. Greater delivery of vaccination is highly cost-effective and has the potential to significantly reduce childhood deaths from pneumonia and diarrhoea (Feikin et al, 2016). Vaccination strategies depend on mass coverage. Both demand- and supply-side approaches (for example, mass communication or changes through health systems) have been used to increase vaccine delivery. While noting the central importance of vaccine supply and distribution, one review also took into account the demand side and argued that this was important to overcome obstacles that could disadvantage the poorest. The review suggests that both education and financial incentives are effective at increasing use, but places more emphasis on education, and shows that knowledge-based approaches are most important (Johri et al, 2016). Of those strategies seeking to improve vaccination rates, the success of face-to-face interventions aimed at increasing knowledge is low (the review argues for routine vaccination through existing health service activities, not new channels; Kaufman et al, 2013). A second review identifies that while targeting communities to increase knowledge could be successful (for example, via community meetings), it is also resource-intensive and so should be focused on communities with low coverage rates (Saeterdal et al, 2014).

Quality early learning programmes support later schooling

Studies conducted across the world (including Young Lives studies) attest to the benefits of early learning programmes for 3- to 5-year-olds affected by poverty, which include improvements in cognitive and psychosocial skills. All things considered, children from low-income backgrounds attending formal preschools each day of the week benefit more than those participating in more informal, irregular approaches. It is the quality of teaching and learning that makes the difference and this is independent of who delivers the programme. There is broad agreement that a holistic curriculum that encourages the development of gross and fine motor skills, language and mathematics skills, cognition and executive functioning, and socio-emotional wellbeing is necessary if children are to be ready to enter formal schooling. In addition, a play-based approach to learning with sufficient resources, teachers who interact sensitively with their children, and culturally appropriate teacher–child ratios are key indicators of ECCE programme quality. The teacher's ability to help support children's development to higher levels of understanding and performance is a central ingredient. While training to work with this age group is essential, higher teacher qualifications are not necessarily associated with better-quality programmes (Biersteker et al, 2016).

While there is an excellent case for scaling up access to early learning programmes in the years prior to school (Nores and Barnett, 2010; Engle et al, 2011), there are many challenges to ensuring that this will be done well, particularly in countries with limited resources (Woodhead et al, 2017). It is even a considerable challenge in the United States, as Farran and Lipsey (2015) recount. If we do not pay attention to quality of delivery, resources will be wasted on high access to poor-quality programmes, with disappointing results. As Britto and colleagues stress: 'If we are to achieve equity in child outcomes within and across nations, the solution lies not just in increasing access, but in improving quality' (2011, p 3).

Scaling access to quality early learning opportunities in LMICs requires policy-makers to step back and undertake a considered scoping of their environment and its possibilities for early learning programme support and delivery. Difficult questions must be asked. For example, is it better for the state to spend limited funds on enhancing the quality of teaching and learning in the reception year of public schools, over which the public sector has control, and leave the non-profit sector to address the learning needs of preschool children? Or do governments decide that they have the capacity to fund and support quality delivery in both the public school system and at the preschool level (as, for example, in Vietnam)?

Supporting mothers is part of supporting children's development

Poverty is associated with increased risk of common mental health problems such as anxiety and depression among women through 'social exclusion, high stressors, reduced social capital, malnutrition, obstetric risks and increased risk of violence and trauma' (Lund et al, 2010, p 526). In addition, people with mental health problems may be at increased risk of becoming poor. As these authors point out, most studies are cross-sectional, but there is evidence for the first pathway from longitudinal investigations. Poverty is not good for mental health. Either way, ongoing psychological distress, and particularly depression, reduces the capacity to provide adequate care and stimulation, and is associated with increased likelihood of growth stunting and other negative developmental outcomes (Wachs et al, 2009; Wachs and Rahman, 2013; Tredoux and Dawes, 2018). Given these findings and their cost to young children and to society through loss of potential, it is increasingly recognised that policies are needed to address the needs of mothers of young children with mental health challenges. Mental health services tend to receive limited policy attention and resources in LMICs. The first step is to recognise the problem. Epidemiological surveys are needed to draw the attention of health ministries to the scale of the problem, and to aid policy formulation and planning for service delivery. This should include mental health screening at the primary health level (Vythilingum et al, 2013).

Upstream interventions would include reducing the main environmental risk factor – poverty – itself and at the individual level, promoting interventions to provide psychosocial support – and mental health services, where necessary – to affected women (Araya et al, 2003). A few promising models of psychosocial support and intervention for vulnerable mothers in LMICs (such as cognitive-behavioural therapy), usually through the primary health system, are emerging. These are normally delivered by trained community health workers and depending on the intervention, improvements in maternal wellbeing and child outcomes are evident (Cooper et al, 2002; Rahman et al, 2008; Wachs et al, 2009). Such interventions are particularly important during pregnancy and the first two years of life, when mothers are particularly vulnerable to post-natal depression and other conditions, and the impact on children's growth and intellectual development is particularly significant.

Conclusion

Since 2000, it has been increasingly recognised that early childhood is a critical window in the life course. The MDGs focused on child survival and early health, and the SDGs have broadened that vision with attention to early childhood development and preschool.

Young Lives findings draw attention to the central importance of context in shaping early childhood, each of the different layers highlighted in the bioecological framework playing a part. The findings point to the usefulness of this framework in understanding the sources of influence that bear on early development in the household environment (food, water sanitation and adequate care), local community institutions (health services) and high-quality, holistic early learning programmes), all the way up to macro-level policies.

Stunting is a consequence of the disease, care and food security environment the child lives in. Poverty is a central risk factor. The Young Lives countries show progress in stunting reduction, notably in Peru where reducing under-nutrition has been given national importance. The ongoing prevalence of stunting nevertheless is a clear channel through which poverty in childhood results in disadvantaged development. Overcoming early under-nutrition is important to school readiness and school performance in the primary years, to which we turn in the next chapter. The association between early life under-nutrition and impaired cognitive development, as well as lower psychosocial wellbeing, indicates how early deprivation can set a child on a negative development cascade. As disadvantages tend to have cumulative effects, this trend becomes increasingly difficult to reverse as children grow older, hence the emphasis on interventions starting as early as possible, including through enhanced maternal health and wellbeing.

Interventions to improve early childhood circumstances have been shown to work for the poorest children. Nutritional supplementation has been found to support healthy growth, especially for young children and poorer children. Interventions to support infants also have the potential to support mothers and primary caregivers. The greatest long-term gains require attention to quality, and so this needs to be built into delivery and monitoring systems.

As these findings suggest, to ensure their survival, health and development, young children need a multi-sectoral response (involving the health, education and social sectors). In scaling up services to young children (in all sectors), governments are faced with choices about how to use the mechanisms most appropriate to their context, considering available resources. For such services to help reduce the consequences of poverty, they must reach poor children, who are often those most likely to be excluded.

Notes

[1] Study evidence on this is discussed in greater depth by Benny and colleagues (2018).

[2] Stunting is defined as being shorter than two standard deviations below the WHO norm. It is expected that in a normal population, 2.5% of children would fall below that level and so higher rates of stunting than this suggest chronic under-nutrition (see Benny et al, 2018).

[3] To give some sense of scale, in a normal (population) distribution, 68% of individual report results lie within one standard deviation of the sample average, a large amount.

[4] Cueto and colleagues (2015) find that the benefit of centre-based preschool was higher for children who had better growth indicators in infancy, suggesting that without good nutrition preschool could magnify existing gaps.

FIVE

Middle childhood: A key time for healthy development and learning

This chapter focuses on middle childhood, a crucial time in children's development following the dramatic advances of early childhood, and preceding the dynamic processes of pubertal and social change during adolescence. Skills and values developed during middle childhood build on foundations established in early childhood and set the stage for adolescence. Thus, it is vital that the momentum established in the early years is sustained through this important life phase. The influence of the family remains strong in this period, but new experiences and stimuli come into play as boys and girls participate in a wider range of social and institutional settings, most prominent among these being school.

Young Lives evidence presented in this chapter shows that children's growth trajectories are more dynamic during middle childhood than is often recognised. This finding suggests a wider policy opportunity. Currently, policies that address child nutrition and growth attend mainly to early childhood, and the first 1,000 days of life has been the prime focus (see UNICEF, 2015), as indicated in Chapter Four. However, the Sustainable Development Goal (SDG) target 2.2 commits further to a reduction in stunting in the first five years (see UNGA, 2017). Young Lives evidence presented in the chapter confirms these priorities, but also identifies the potential for growth recovery in middle childhood. This adds new hope, especially since recovery can be linked with cognitive gains. Given the global scale of under-nutrition, the findings of post-infancy growth recovery and faltering are among the most important generated by Young Lives.

The transition from early to middle childhood is marked by the start of school, in contemporary societies the single most important institutional milestone for children in this phase. This transition is vital for learning, the activities associated with schooling also contributing significantly to children's physical, social and emotional development, and their ideas about future goals and prospects. School is central to children's time use and is a potential delivery channel for other services, particularly health and nutrition. Nevertheless, impressive advances in access across most low- and middle-income countries

(LMICs) in recent decades mask a lack of progress on education quality, the consensus among many lead organisations internationally being that there is a learning crisis in basic skills (for example, UNESCO, 2013; International Commission on Financing Global Education Opportunity, 2018; The World Bank, 2018b). SDG 4 recognises these concerns through a focus on 'inclusive and equitable quality education'. Young Lives findings presented in this chapter identify opportunities and constraints to children's learning. They highlight factors associated with home background as well as those due to school systems, and showing how early disadvantage is compounded through middle childhood, driving a negative developmental cascade. Focusing on ways to achieve equitable education is therefore also a strategy to improve the quality of learning. The findings also show that within the global learning crisis there are very different national stories. In Ethiopia and United Andhra Pradesh, few children gain basic skills, whereas in Peru and Vietnam, performance is better in overall terms, although equity remains an important concern.

Early nutrition is crucial but later growth recovery and faltering is evident

This section confirms the importance of early growth in height-for-age predicting children's subsequent growth and development and highlights how middle childhood nutrition and health is crucial for consolidating advances made in early childhood. Yet it also shares striking evidence of the considerable dynamism in children's growth through the middle childhood years and into adolescence, with some Young Lives children recovering in growth following earlier deficits, and others faltering after normal initial growth. Analysing the potential for post-infancy recovery in growth requires caution for methodological reasons (see Appendix 2). Nevertheless, Young Lives evidence indicates that early growth status does not necessarily fix children's later growth and development trajectories, signalling the potential for important remedial intervention.

As indicated in the previous chapter, changes in children's growth trajectories during middle childhood can be shown using stunting as the indicator. When growth faltering and recovery are discussed, these relate to children's relative growth, assessed against the norm defined by the World Health Organization (WHO) for the child's age and sex (see Benny et al, 2018). Across the four countries, around half of those children who were stunted at age one (that is, in infancy), were found not to be stunted by age 8 (Georgiadis and Penny, 2017). Figure 5.1

illustrates the pattern for ages 1 to 15 years in United Andhra Pradesh, since the pattern is similar to those of the other countries. It shows that some children whose growth was stunted in early childhood were recovering and others whose early growth was normal had begun to falter through middle childhood and even into early adolescence.

The obvious question that arises from this evidence is whether these changes are real and, if so, important. The measure used in Figure 5.1 relies on the threshold that defines stunting status, so some of the changes in growth status may reflect quite small real changes above or below this threshold, or indeed be due to measurement or other sources of error. The average underlying changes are, however, substantial, making such explanations unlikely. Comparing changes over the period, those children who recovered from initial stunting between ages 1 and 8 years saw an increase in height-for-age Z (HAZ) scores of 1.08 and 1.88, for Vietnam and Ethiopia respectively. Those whose growth faltered saw their average HAZ score fall by between

Figure 5.1: Stunting trajectories over childhood, India (UAP) Younger Cohort

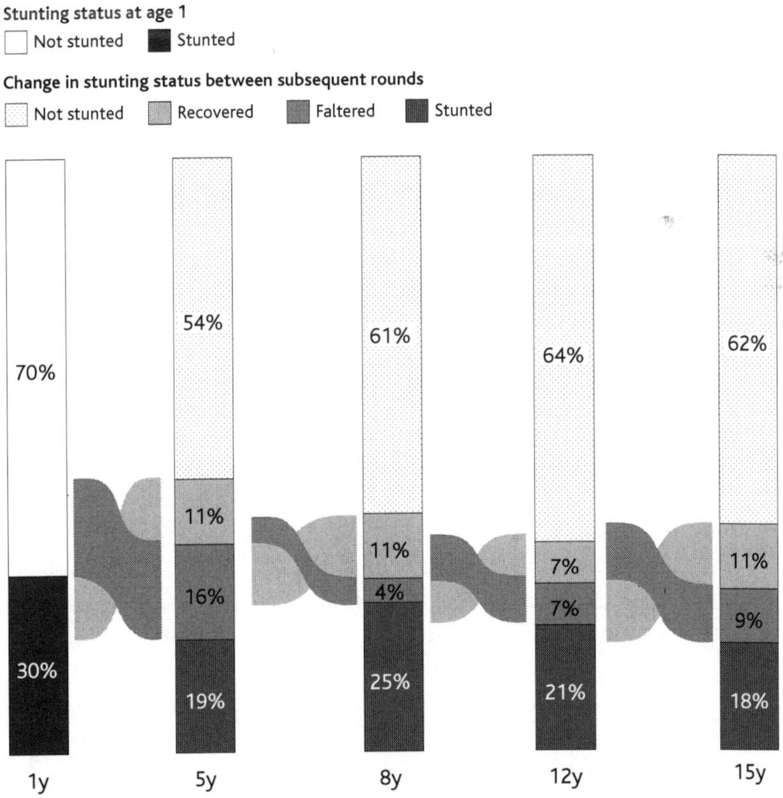

Stunting status at age 1
☐ Not stunted   ■ Stunted

Change in stunting status between subsequent rounds
Not stunted   Recovered   Faltered   Stunted

0.85 and 1.45, for Ethiopia and Peru respectively (Crookston et al, 2013; see also Dornan and Georgiadis, 2015).

The potential for recovery depends on a child's circumstances (see the following section) and the extent and timing of early-life stunting. In United Andhra Pradesh children who were more severely stunted were less likely to recover, with 44% overall of those stunted as infants recovering by 5 years of age, compared with only 20% of those who were severely stunted (that is, with height-for-age below three standard deviations). Of those who were stunted at 5 years, overall 35% had recovered by age 8, compared with only 8% of those who were severely stunted (Singh et al, 2017). This evidence can be read to emphasise the central importance of prevention, but it does not suggest that severely stunted children cannot recover and many do despite the severity of stunting (see Crookston et al, 2010 for Peru, and Benny et al, 2018 for a wider discussion).[1]

Physical recovery is linked to better cognitive scores, but those who were never stunted do best of all

Stunting is predictive of neurological development and has therefore become a prominent indicator of children's broader wellbeing. What is most exciting about the Young Lives finding on growth dynamism in middle childhood, therefore, is that recovery in linear growth has been found to be linked with better performance in language and numeracy tests. Middle childhood gains in either height or cognition may change the trajectories of affected children from a negative to a positive developmental cascade (see, for example, Crookston et al, 2013; Georgiadis and Penny, 2017; Georgiadis et al, 2017).

Georgiadis and colleagues (2017) explore the relationship between recovery from stunting in early childhood and receptive vocabulary and maths test performance at age 8 and 12. The authors compared different trajectories of change in stunting status at 5, 8 and 12 years. This analysis informs us about the timing of when recovery matters most. The patterns described here are common to the four countries. In tests of receptive vocabulary and mathematics, children with *no* history of stunting always performed better than children whose growth was stunted at some point in early childhood. Those who remained stunted from age 1 through 12 years performed worse than those with normal growth, those who recovered at some point, and those who faltered. This corroborates evidence from other studies that consistent stunting compromises cognitive development the most. Gains in cognitive development are higher for those whose recovery took place earlier – before five years of age – and was then sustained. While these findings do not necessarily imply a causal relation between normal height-for-age and elevated test scores, they signal that the circumstances that trigger improved physical development also have positive consequences for learning. While this is encouraging, it remains important to note that gains are smaller at older ages than younger ones (Georgiadis and Penny, 2017; Georgiadis et al, 2017).

The predictors of growth recovery and faltering include poverty

The Young Lives study design allows identification of earlier determinants of change in height growth, and captures the reflections of children and families on how nutrition and food security might be contributory. Identifying the factors predicting change in growth trajectories and the likelihood of these factors being affected by intervention is extremely important for policy.

Maternal height, poverty, social protection measures and community infrastructure, especially sanitation and health services, are all linked with post-infancy recovery in children's growth (Dornan and Georgiadis, 2015). Therefore, it is to be expected that recovery is most likely when the mother is healthy (as indicated by her height), the household does not experience poverty, and has access to both social protection (where needed) and strong basic services. A comprehensive analysis has been undertaken of the factors linked to change in height growth during the two middle childhood periods, from 5 to 8 and 8 to 12 years, and findings that are significant in two or more countries are reproduced here (Georgiadis et al, 2017). During the earlier middle childhood phase – 5 to 8 years – individual factors linked with reduced chances of recovery include sex (boys being less likely to recover), birth order (its impact differing between countries) and age (older children being less likely to recover). Having a taller mother and greater household wealth was associated with an increased chance of recovery. Community factors included rubbish collection by truck, an indicator of community cleanliness and disease risk, and health facilities. The factors associated with physical recovery in the later middle childhood period – 8 to 12 years – are similar to those that apply in the earlier phase, though birth order, availability of a health facility and maternal education were not shown to be important in this later period. In later middle childhood (by 12 years), the age of onset of puberty is also important. In the short term, an early growth spurt may appear as height recovery, but as Chapter Six discusses, in the longer term late onset puberty allows a longer window for growth.

Experiencing a natural disaster, and higher prices of goods and food, are also linked with reduced recovery (though it may simply be that natural disasters occurred during this period rather than that they were necessarily more important during later middle childhood).

The dynamism in children's growth during middle childhood also reflects the ongoing volatility of livelihoods and food supply in many Young Lives households. By the time children reach middle childhood, they are aware just how central nutrition is to their physical growth and wider development and wellbeing, although, unsurprisingly, volume and frequency of food consumption is often given more attention than nutrient quality. Mihretu, from Ethiopia, stated that 'to live well, children need to get a balanced diet' (quoted in Morrow et al, 2017, p 4). Other children noted the importance of 'good food' in their recovery from illness (Morrow et al, 2017, p 4). In terms of the implications for education, Krishna, a nine-year-old boy, said, 'We need to study. We need to answer the question, and we must eat well … if we eat well, we can study' (quoted in Aurino and Morrow, 2018, p 219).

Children are particularly worried by food insecurity, which in Young Lives sites frequently results from food shortages and/or increases in food prices associated with extreme weather events, market instability or other economic shocks. Families and households may try to lessen the negative impacts of such shocks, although, as indicated in Chapter Four, sometimes the adverse consequences for children's nutrition cannot be avoided. Louam – the youngest of seven children – comes from a rural Ethiopian village. Her family farm and breed cattle. They used to be relatively well off, but when interviewed at 6 years old, Louam said they had had a very difficult year as their crops failed due to drought. She explained: 'We sold our animals and had to buy grain. We sold nine sheep and also our eucalyptus trees' (quoted in van der Gaag et al, 2012, p 13). For her, poverty signified wearing ragged clothes and going hungry. Louam's mother confirmed that things were bad at this time and that there was insufficient food for the children so the family lived on bread and tea: 'She lost weight and became thin but now she improves, with the help of God. She eats a variety of food and a balanced diet' (quoted in Knowles and van der Gaag, 2009, p 14). It is not uncommon for Young Lives children to go hungry. As shown in Chapter Four, when food stocks are low, parents reduce the number of meals and portion sizes, though both children and adults are aware that this undermines children's ability to work or concentrate in school (Aurino and Morrow, 2018, p 219). In middle childhood, many children collaborate actively with their families in alleviating food insecurity through work. Defar, in Ethiopia, explained that during rainy seasons, when food is scarce and the family goes hungry, 'my grandmother and me survive selling eucalyptus seed' (quoted in Morrow et al, 2017, p 5). Other families sell their possessions to buy food.

There has been far less policy attention to nutrition, growth and health in middle childhood than there has been to education. Recognition of the importance of growth dynamism for children's wider development during this phase opens up new policy opportunities. Of the predictors of changes in growth status, some are amenable to policy intervention, for example, improving basic services, social protection and other community conditions. Using school as a platform for enhancing children's nutrition and development can also bring immediate gains. The midday meal programme in schools in United Andhra Pradesh, in particular, has been shown to support growth recovery in children who have experienced drought (Singh et al, 2014).

Schooling dominates children's lives during middle childhood

Primary school education has become the single most important defining feature of middle childhood across LMICs, reflecting a strong policy focus on education globally. In the Young Lives countries, government schools have traditionally dominated education delivery, especially for the most disadvantaged communities. Efforts to expand school coverage have led to substantial enrolment gains. These advances are, in turn, associated with high education ambitions. While there is more to be done, children's experience of schooling is now central to understanding their current wellbeing, hopes for the future, and long-term life chances.

Figure 5.2 tracks school enrolment by cohort, age and sex in all four study countries and shows an upward trend.[2] The line tracks the enrolment rate for both the Older and Younger Cohorts. The bubble size depicts sex differences, with larger bubbles indicating larger gaps. The colour indicates the direction of the gap. In United Andhra Pradesh, Peru and Vietnam, enrolment during middle childhood was already comparatively high for the Older Cohort, with higher enrolment in the primary than in the secondary years. In these countries, enrolment and years spent in school either remained high, or increased, for the Younger Cohort. The age of school entry is later in Ethiopia than the other countries, but even so, the Younger

Figure 5.2: Education enrolment by age, and enrolment gaps by gender

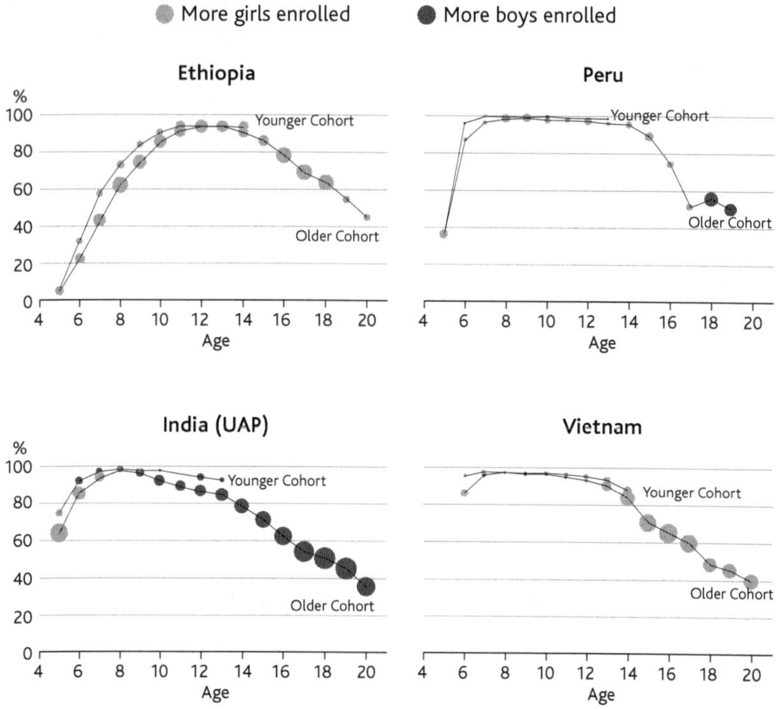

More girls enrolled   More boys enrolled

Note: Area of circle is proportional to the size of gender gap.

Source: Data for this visualisation is taken from Older and Younger Cohort individuals present in all rounds of the Young Lives survey

Cohort in Ethiopia started school on average half a year earlier (at age 7.1 years) than did the Older Cohort (age 7.6 years). Comparing the Ethiopian cohorts shows an average increase from 66% to 77% enrolment at age 8. Strikingly, this was driven by a rapid increase in enrolment in rural areas, up from 51 to 69%, likely to be a result of earlier – that is, on time – enrolment (Woldehanna et al, 2011).

Figure 5.2 also shows that, perhaps surprisingly, in Ethiopia and Vietnam girls are more likely to be enrolled than boys. In Peru, there is a high overall enrolment rate and little difference by gender. In United Andhra Pradesh, more boys are enrolled than girls, and this difference accelerates through adolescence; although the pattern remained pro-boy across the two cohorts, there was a narrowing of the gap between the Older and Younger Cohorts. This change coincided with implementation of the Right to Education Act (in 2009), which, among other aims, sought to extend the school-leaving age.

Examination of children's use of time confirms the dominance of school and studying during middle childhood (see Espinoza-Revollo and Porter, 2018). Figure 5.3 presents the data for Ethiopia on boys' and girls' time use on a typical school day, indicating the changes as they pass through middle childhood and adolescence. While the overall pattern for the four countries is similar, Ethiopian children tend to report less time in schooling and studying than in the other countries. Data are disaggregated by the wealth of households, with

Figure 5.3: Time spent on studying at school and home on a typical school day, Ethiopia

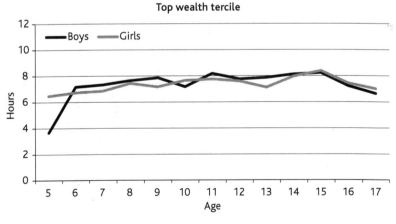

Note: These percentages are for school and preschool (which explains the hours of study noted prior to formal school start at 7 years).

Source: Data for this visualisation is taken from Younger Cohort households in round 5 of the Young Lives survey

children in the top wealth tercile separated out from children in the bottom tercile.[3] Boys and girls report similar levels of engagement with education. But the poorest children spend less time at school and studying than the least poor, especially at younger ages, having been much less likely to attend preschool and often joined school later.

Mass school enrolment has not been matched by equal learning gains

Despite impressive enrolment during middle childhood, levels of learning remain very low in many LMICs. Young Lives evidence confirms this trend, indicating that the challenge of raising basic skill levels is considerable. This is about both children's background disadvantages and weak school systems. However, the degree to which education reform is needed varies enormously both between and within countries.[4] The challenge is greatest in Ethiopia and United Andhra Pradesh, where basic skill attainment is low, and less so in Peru and Vietnam, where children's performance is somewhat better. Figure 5.4 shows the wide variation in how many children in each country sample could read a very simple sentence at age 8.

Figure 5.4: Reading levels at age 8 (Older Cohort age 8 = 2002, Younger Cohort age 8 = 2009)

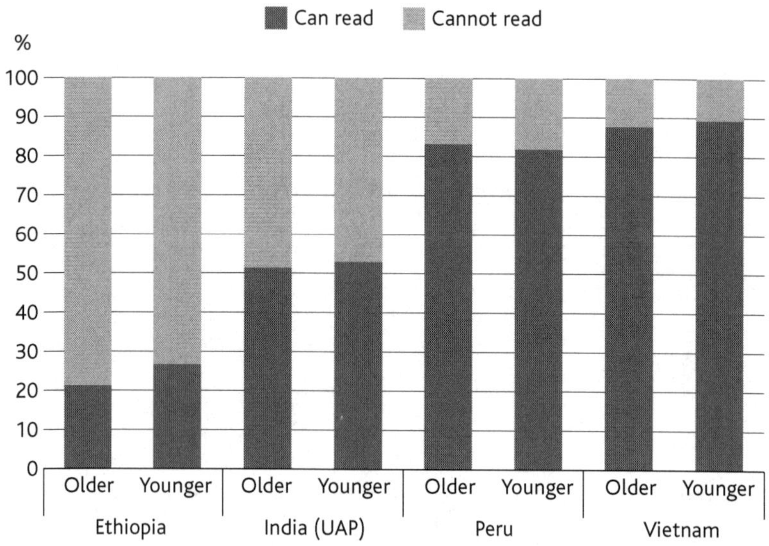

Source: Rossiter et al (2018)

Achieving good basic skills implies tackling major within-country differences in learning

Behind the low average learning in children's basic skills there lie substantial within-country differences in cognitive achievement. Chapter Four showed that inequalities in basic skills are apparent in all four countries even at 5 years of age, prior to school entry. Evidence presented here shows that such disparities persist and in some cases become more marked through middle childhood. Vietnam outperforms the other three countries on basic skills, but even in Vietnam there are serious learning inequalities, as noted in the next section. Raising the performance of the most marginalised children is a key step in raising skills to an acceptable level across the board. This section considers some of the key individual, household and community factors associated with school attainment. School systems are discussed in the next section.

Individual aptitude undoubtedly plays a role, but as discussed in Chapters Two and Seven, much is also likely due to the child's environment. As with other indicators of wellbeing and development, the poorest children, those living in rural areas, those whose parents are the least educated, and those belonging to ethnic, language or religious minority groups, usually score less well than their peers. Very often these children lag behind because of disadvantageous home circumstances that undermine their schooling. For example, they are likely to be more prone to illness and under-nutrition, to work, and enjoy less learning support at home than their better-off peers. But children in the same country and even those in the same schools may have very different experiences of education. Figure 5.5 shows a typical pattern, for maths achievement in United Andhra Pradesh by the end of middle childhood (at age 12). The figure shows differences based on gender, household wealth and rural and urban location.

Early performance on learning indicators is predictive of later success (Cueto et al, 2016; see also Rossiter et al, 2018, and Chapter Seven). The positive developmental cascade of early advantage starts very young, leading to school readiness and later success. Early performance (both bad and good) can be further enhanced or undermined by circumstances through middle childhood. Unpicking which of many home background and educational influences acts as the greatest drain on learning is a challenge, given that multiple factors are at play. For example, while there are clear differences in achievement between minority and majority ethnic and language groups in Vietnam, Peru and United Andhra Pradesh, the underlying reasons are not

Figure 5.5: Maths achievement test (Younger Cohort age 12, India [UAP])

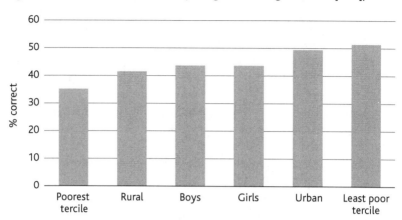

immediately evident. Children from minority backgrounds may experience greater barriers in school to learning. But minority status is also a proxy for other disadvantages, such as low levels of parental education and household poverty, and these too may be contributory.

One study found an analytic way through this complexity, by decomposing the sources of the differences in learning on maths and vocabulary tests between children from minority and majority ethnic groups in Vietnam (Glewwe et al, 2015). That analysis shows that differences in test scores are often quite large and exist at 5 years and so cannot be attributed to schooling alone; indeed the largest sources of the difference at age 12 years were household factors. Minority children are likely to be much poorer and have less well-educated parents than their majority counterparts (Glewwe et al, 2015). Other smaller sources of the difference included whether children spent more time in school and less in work, and had better nutrition, both of which could also reflect household economic status (Glewwe et al, 2015).

Household constraints, including children assisting with domestic and other chores, often result in irregular attendance, which weakens attention to studies and progress through school, and may lead to early school departure. In Ethiopia, for example, among children enrolled in grade 4 (typically aged 11-12), 87% were found to be present in the school when researchers visited during the primary school survey, and in parts of the rural Somali region attendance was just under half of those registered (Aurino et al, 2014, p 13). Often children start assisting with family duties at around age 4 to 6 years, which is also the age they begin school. This form of work is one of the main contributors to irregular attendance, and may lead to late entry into school, especially in rural areas of Ethiopia. It also diminishes concentration in school (Tafere and Pankhurst, 2015; see also Chapter Six). The type and amount of work undertaken by children, and the trade-off between work and school, is shaped by a child's gender and age. The gendered division of labour is normally more flexible in middle childhood than in adolescence (Heissler and Porter, 2013; Chuta, 2014; Crivello and van der Gaag, 2016). At very young ages, children's work usually involves light chores in the home and/or the family enterprise, and is as much about learning life skills as it is helping their families. However, poorer children generally feel an obligation to work regardless of their age. Ramya, a 12-year-old girl in United Andhra Pradesh, explains the weight of responsibility that children commonly feel when it comes to supporting their families through work:

> We have raised loans, and we will have to repay the loans.... Father took a loan for our sisters' marriage. [Two sisters were married on the same day the previous year.] We have taken a loan of 1 lakh rupees [approximately £1,000] for their marriage.... I have to work, though it is hard work; we have to clear the loans. (Quoted in Morrow et al, 2014 p 152)

The pressures of combining school and work generally intensify as children grow older, this being most apparent at around age 12; many boys in particular also start doing paid work between ages 9 and 10, sometimes alongside unpaid chores in the home (Morrow et al, 2014; Crivello and van der Gaag, 2016). The demands of work also rise at times of peak labour demand, such as during the planting and harvesting seasons. Household composition often affects the time allocation between school and work, as the gender balance of the sibling group, birth order, and work capacity of adults can all play a part (Heissler and Porter, 2013). Sessen, from Ethiopia, explained:

> I started working when I was very small. I was herding the livestock because I was the last-born child in the family and we did not have a boy. At the time, after observing my friends going to school, I wanted to start school. I started going to school, but I also wished to work. Finally, I opted to work.... I stopped school when my father died and my mother had no-one to help her. I decided to help her by doing some work for pay. (Quoted in Tafere and Chuta, 2016, p 11)

Although work can be burdensome and sometimes competes with schooling, it may also facilitate learning of important life and pro-social skills (Morrow and Boyden, 2018). For many of the children from poorer families, undertaking paid work makes school attendance for them or their younger siblings possible by helping fund the costs of school materials, uniforms and transport to and from school. For example, Hadush, in Ethiopia, was the only boy in a household, and the youngest of eight siblings. He herded cattle full-time, so that his sisters could attend school. Mihretu was able to attend school only because his two elder brothers herded the cattle (Boyden et al, 2016). The implications of children's care and economic work for their learning during adolescence are discussed in Chapter Six.

Different school systems produce different learning opportunities for different groups of children

Learning inequalities are not just about home background or individual capacity, since national education systems produce both different average learning levels and inequity. Some systems are likely to exacerbate learning differences if the poor and the less poor, minorities and the majority, attend different schools, or are treated differently in the same school. For example, in Vietnam, ethnic minority children confront multiple challenges at school. Foremost among these is language of instruction, which from entry onwards is Vietnamese. This greatly disadvantages monolingual minority children, as evidenced by the fact that they performed less well in tests than those minority children who either spoke Vietnamese, or lived in mixed communities. In the case of the H'Roi ethnic group, one Young Lives interviewer noted that families often did not teach their children Vietnamese because they said the children would learn to speak the language in school (Vu, 2014). However, a 9-year-old boy named Y Sinh had only attended school for a few days in his life, so he could only speak H'Roi, and was unfamiliar with the Vietnamese alphabet. Rather than attend school, Y Sinh worked to earn money to feed the family, showing the dramatic impact that both poverty and language barriers can have on education (van der Gaag et al 2012). Stories such as Y Sinh's represent an important supplement to the otherwise positive and comparatively equitable story that emerges from analysis of the Vietnamese primary school system discussed in this section. Over the post-2000 period, data from Vietnam suggest substantial progress in narrowing gaps between ethnic minority and ethnic majority children (Dang and Glewwe, 2017). It is therefore hoped that Y Sinh's experience reflects the situation as it was in the past, but nevertheless it illustrates the challenges involved in ensuring schooling reaches all children.

Although Young Lives samples are not nationally representative, and care is needed in making comparisons (see Chapter Two), the contrast in primary schooling between Peru and Vietnam is instructive. As noted earlier, these two countries generally perform better on learning indicators than do Ethiopia and United Andhra Pradesh. Yet they differ notably in terms of equity during middle childhood, particularly in basic education. Analysis of data from the school-effectiveness surveys, administered when children were aged around 10, considered how schools in the two countries affected children's learning (Krutikova et al, 2014). In Peru, children who were more advantaged, such as by having a more educated mother, or coming from a wealthier background, did better than less advantaged children at the same schools. In Vietnam, no such difference was identified, suggesting greater equity, which the authors attribute to a focus on ensuring all children reach a 'minimum standard' of learning (Krutikova et al, 2014). In Peru, a close link was identified between a child's background, the preschool facility attended at age 1, and systematic differences in opportunities to learn at age 12 (Cueto et al, 2014).

The school-effectiveness survey in Vietnam, which tracked the performance of Younger Cohort children and their peers from the start to the end of grade 5, indicates that the education system is both productive and comparatively equitable. This was evident by comparing test results at the start and end of the year. Figure 5.6 provides the scores for mathematics aggregated at the school level (similar findings were identified in Vietnam for reading). The baseline (0) is the average expected, with those schools above the line (to the right of the chart) 'adding more value',[5] and those below adding less value.

The figure shows that differences between primary schools are large. The difference between the top and bottom third of schools ranked by how much they added value was equivalent to the average gain over the whole of grade five. Raising the impact of the schools on the left of the chart could therefore increase average performance considerably. But given that Vietnam is a good performer on both equity and productivity, it is very likely that even larger differences between schools exist across school systems in other countries that perform less well. Encouragingly, there was little evidence that the most disadvantaged children were in the lowest-performing schools; indeed children from minority backgrounds (who started the school

Figure 5.6: School value added during grade 5 in maths, Vietnam

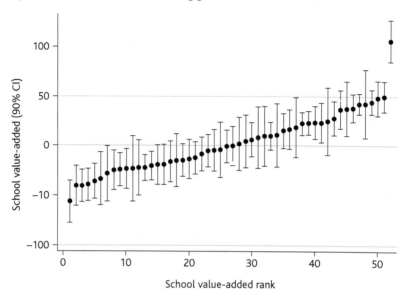

Note: Each point is a school, ranked by the value added. The bars above and below the point are the 90% confidence interval.

Source: Rolleston et al (2013, Figure 18)

year far behind) caught up in their learning, narrowing gaps with their more advantaged peers against the curricular expectation over the school year. This pattern of comparative equity contrasts sharply with the situation in Peru noted earlier.

The investigators considered what might account for the variation in value added in the Vietnam schools. This analysis is associative, not causal, but still helps understanding of the characteristics of effective schools and classes (see Rolleston et al, 2013, p 37, Table 15). High-performing schools had better facilities, including separate rooms for each class and working electricity, and a higher proportion of teachers with a degree. The school principals came from the province where the school is based, and were less likely to admit all pupils who applied (the stated application criteria being area of residence). Both high- and low-value-added schools included pupils who were less advantaged than the sample as a whole, and minority pupils actually made up a larger proportion in the high-performing than the low-performing schools.

The same study analysed differences at the classroom level. This is more informative than school-level analysis, which aggregated data from classes. Differences in the value added to children's learning were identified by examining the contribution of classroom characteristics. The role of household background factors was examined, making it possible to assess whether disadvantaged pupils faced greater learning challenges than their wealthier counterparts (see Rolleston et al, 2013, p 39, Table 16). Important differences were again identified between low- and high-performing classes; the latter had better classroom infrastructure and teaching resources, and better trained teachers, who reported greater levels of commitment to teaching. Teachers in high-performing classes were more likely to have permanent contracts and less likely to come from the province in which they were teaching. They also had more evaluations in the previous year, and were less likely to have additional work outside school. Those teaching higher-value-added classes tended to display higher levels of efficacy (which suggests teachers think they can make a difference), and were less likely to believe that home background dominates children's ability to learn. In high-value-added classes, teachers also reported children as having a higher general ability and higher ability in maths and Vietnamese specifically, though differences in test scores at the start of the year between high- and low-value-added schools are small or non-existent. Finally, pupils in high-value-added classes spent more time in extra classes, and high-performing classes had fewer grade repeaters. There was no significant difference in the home background or the proportion of minority ethnic students between high- and low-value-added classes.

Harsh school environments and inflexibility undermine access and learning

Most discussions and most measures of school systems focus on topics seen as directly affecting learning, such as curriculum content, pedagogy and governance. Less attention is paid to the contribution of the wider school environment. Young Lives has explored children's experiences of the school context, including their perceptions of school facilities such as the hygiene and privacy of the toilets, and exposure to bullying and corporal punishment, all of which can affect both learning and attendance. In Ethiopia, children identified unsanitary pit latrines as having a constant negative impact on their experience of school. For example, one girl explained that the punishment for being late is often to clean the toilets, and said: 'If I am late, I would rather go back home than clean a toilet ... because I might have been sick with a flu because of the bad smell of the toilet (quoted in Cameron, 2009, p 9). Other children complained that students and teachers tend to defecate outside of the toilet because it is dirty and they fear falling in the hole, this in turn causing the toilet block to smell and to attract flies, triggering illness. As a result of these conditions, many children prefer to defecate in open fields or woods near the school.

Violence and social exclusion are other concerns for many pupils during the middle childhood years. For example, minority ethnic children in Vietnam report being stigmatised and bullied by their peers. Similar findings are evident in Peru. Ames and Rojas (2010) describe the experience of Eva, a Quechua-speaking child from a rural community. Eva attended school in the district capital, which was a half-hour drive, or a three-hour walk when no public transportation was available. She described feeling marginalised by her classmates because she came from a rural village. Other students would tease her, calling her 'indigenous' as an insult. She reported having no friends at school, and spending breaks playing with a cousin. On the other hand, her mother explained that when Eva returned home to the village, she would show off, act superior to local girls, and refuse to speak Quechua or wear traditional shawls.

Despite corporal punishment in school being formally prohibited in all four countries, many children described being hit by teachers and parents, as well as experiencing fighting or bullying between peers. Young Lives evidence shows that experiencing corporal punishment at age 8 is associated with lower maths scores at 12, having controlled for other background characteristics. Modelling across the four countries has been used to show that the effects are significant. The extent of the underlying association between corporal punishment and lower maths scores is of equivalent magnitude to the effect associated with the child's caregiver having between three and six years *less* education (Ogando Portela and Pells, 2015b). Boys are more likely to experience corporal punishment than girls. These fears and experiences grow through adolescence and are addressed in Chapter Six.

Caregivers have varying reactions to the use of corporal punishment in schools. Some believe in strong discipline as a way of improving learning. For example, in United Andhra Pradesh, the mother of Sahithi, in class 1, said that the most important quality in a teacher is '[she] should teach well, she should make them disciplined, by beating them if they don't listen' (quoted in Streuli et al, 2011, p 24). However, many complain about corporal punishment as being ineffective and merely instilling fear. Children mirror these views. In Poompuhar, in United Andhra Pradesh, Vishnu described his experiences in a private primary school:

YL: What will she do if you answered wrong?

Vishnu: She hits us … if we shout and don't tell (the answer). If we answer then she won't hit.

YL: Is it good to hit or not?

Vishnu: No, they should not hit. We do learn; should not beat us.

YL: What happens if you are beaten?

Vishnu: It hurts us. We feel like crying. (Quoted in Streuli, et al 2011 pp 47-48)

Many rural girls and boys find that if they miss school to work or care for their families, are late or have not completed homework, their schools take an inflexible and punitive approach, which may involve violence or exclusion. Those affected risk falling behind their classmates as a consequence.

Rising demand for private schools shows improvement is needed in the quality of government schools

In many countries, raised education aspirations, together with poor public sector performance, coexist with the perception that private schools are better than public education. Children's reports of their school experiences bear out quality concerns. Manoj, a boy in class 2 from Poompuhar in United Andhra Pradesh, described his rural government school: 'They don't teach us anything, they ask us to write…. We sit on the floor.' His mother agreed, stating that 'there is nothing at all in the school except for the board … they sit down, on the floor … they don't teach at all, he simply goes, sits there and comes back home' (quoted in Streuli et al, 2011, p 28).

These experiences are reflected in an upsurge in demand for private tutoring and private schooling (Rolleston and Moore, 2018; Rossiter et al, 2018). Of the Young Lives countries, this trend is most evident in United Andhra Pradesh. Comparing the Older and Younger Cohort when participants of each were aged 8 years old showed that over the seven-year period between 2002 and 2009, private school participation had increased from 24% to 44% of children in that country (Woodhead et al, 2013b). Young Lives finds that in United Andhra Pradesh, private schools, particularly those with higher fees, do add greater value than public schools, although the quality is still low (Rolleston and Moore, 2018). A consequence is that the gap between more and less advantaged pupils has widened. Advantaged households are mainly responsible for the rapid upsurge in private primary school enrolment.

Girls, those with older siblings, and those from poorer households or disadvantaged social groups, are less likely to attend a private school (Woodhead et al, 2013b; Singh and Bangay, 2014). As a result, girls and children from less advantaged backgrounds find themselves 'sorted' into schools that are less effective, thereby deepening inequalities over time. This risks significantly increasing the numbers of children denied their right to basic skills.

Yet, some very poor parents buck the trend, making great sacrifices for their children, including daughters, to access private schools. Dilshad, a young girl from a Muslim community in United Andhra Pradesh, lived with her parents and seven brothers in a one-room rented house. Her father was a rickshaw puller, and her mother worked as a maid. Although neither parent had any formal education, they ensured that all of their sons completed school, and sent Dilshad to a private school, despite the cost. Dilshad's mother stated: 'I feel that even if we have to forgo food for one time, we will do that in order to ensure that the children are educated. These days, education is very important' (quoted in Streuli et al, 2011, p 30). They planned to eventually send Dilshad to a government school, but regarded private school as providing a stronger educational foundation in the early years (Streuli et al, 2011, p 30). Jayanthi's experiences highlight similar tensions.

> Jayanthi is 8 years old, studying in 3rd Grade in a rural public school and her father is keen to educate her till Grade VII. The father complains that because the groundnut crop failed, he and his wife have taken up daily wage labour work (Rs 60 per day for men and Rs 50 for women) and have had to borrow money from the local Self Help Group. He shares 'we don't have capacity to admit Jayanthi in a private school ... we have no capacity to pay ... we have to pay Rs 10,000 (per annum) if it is a private residential school ... so we admitted our children in a government school'. (Singh and Bangay, 2014, p 146)

While parents may believe private schools are better, evaluating the impact of such schools requires care. An analysis of the impact among children aged 8-10 years, also taking account of household background, suggests substantial gains to children's learning of English in rural areas, but no effect on maths, nor for either subject in urban areas (Singh, 2014). Tellingly, this analysis concludes that while private schools are considerably cheaper to run than government schools, much of their effect results from catering to children who may already be more advantaged in household background (which itself then predicts learning outcomes), so increasing access to private schools will not raise average learning outcomes substantially. This possibility, combined with equity concerns, suggests private schools do not provide a panacea for low learning levels.

Key findings of what mattered in middle childhood from Young Lives

Young Lives has shown that there is a long window for investment in children's physical growth beyond infancy. Study findings reinforce the dominance of schooling on all aspects of children's lives. To summarise the messages:

- The window for physical growth recovery is longer than often thought. The early years of primary schooling are a particular opportunity to sustain strong growth, through nutrition programmes in schools and other interventions. Where children physically recover, this is supportive of their wider learning.
- Education enrolment has increased substantially in recent decades. Gains have been fastest for the poorest children and for girls. Enrolment and children's time use show the dominance of school in children's lives, although many children combine school with work, which can affect learning and enrolment is not the same as access or quality and basic skills often remain poor and unequal.
- While wide agreement on the challenges of improving education quality is shown in the SDGs, countries face very different productivity and equity challenges. The poorest children are consistently least well prepared even before school, and generally those who do best on early cognitive indicators continue to do better later on. The poorest children frequently also have the worst opportunities to learn. In United Andhra Pradesh, girls are systematically disadvantaged, although in the other countries more gender equity is seen during middle childhood.
- The opportunities to learn experienced by many children are few, due to many factors, including absent teachers, low quality and violent or harsh learning environments. There is more encouraging evidence from Vietnam suggesting both better learning in tests such as maths, and that schools are more equitable there. Minority ethnic children actually caught up relative to more advantaged ethnic

majority children. Evidence from Vietnam shows that trained and motivated teachers can make a difference for children, regardless of background.

• High child and parental aspirations for schooling are demonstrated by rising use of private schooling in United Andhra Pradesh particularly, and these schools appear to add some value even while exacerbating inequities. This evidence highlights the need for significant reform of some public education systems to meet children's demand and right to quality education.

Policy interventions in middle childhood

This section reflects on 'what works' in policies and programmes for children in middle childhood using evidence from beyond the Young Lives study. Policy responses to under-nutrition were discussed in Chapter Four. Therefore, this section addresses other policy areas, starting with social protection, since this is increasingly recognised as fundamental to reducing the constraints to children's wellbeing. It then turns to school and learning, and in the process considers three priority challenges: access to school, improving learning quality and the role of the private sector.

Child-sensitive social protection

Nutrition, health, access to school and academic progress are all affected by poverty. It is now widely recognised that social protection is essential to combat child poverty, and social protection schemes, in particular cash transfers, have increased significantly in recent decades. Financing and coverage for children, however, remain low: the International Labour Organization (ILO) estimates that coverage in Africa as a whole is only 16% (of course, that average masks schemes such as the South African Child Support Grant, which have much higher coverage). Similarly, spending in Africa, Asia and Latin America is below 1% (ILO, 2017, p 11). Thus, the first priority is increased financing and coverage.

There are several approaches. Household-based interventions, such as public works, are not child-focused, but can be important for household economic security. Of the child-focused approaches, conditional cash transfers (CCTs) have emerged as a prominent model in South America, and are increasingly being taken up elsewhere. In recent years, there has been growing attention to unconditional cash transfers (UCTs) in Sub-Saharan Africa (see Handa et al, 2017). Both

CCT and UCT approaches have been found to deliver improvements in children's wellbeing (for example, school attendance). Some have argued that the effect is greater when conditions are enforced (for example, Baird et al, 2013), but other studies have not identified a difference in impact between UCTs and CCTs (Pega et al, 2017). Concerns have also been raised that conditions may exclude those who are least able to comply, but yet may have the greatest need. In an alternative approach, services are linked to cash transfers (for example, by joint delivery or labelling), but without removing benefits from those who are unable to comply (see, for example, Global Coalition to End Child Poverty, 2017). Others have called for a cash-plus approach, whereby transfer programmes are linked to (but not conditional on) complementary services, such as child health, with the suggestion that this combination should increase overall impacts (Roelen, 2017).

Midday meals and other nutrition programmes in schools is an example of an approach that links objectives, in this case social protection, child health and education. With rising enrolment, schools provide an obvious platform for delivery of services with both educational and health benefits, and school meals have been used in many parts of the world to protect children during humanitarian crises (WFP, 2013). While there is consensus that food provided in schools increases educational attendance, there has been more debate over its health benefits. There have also been concerns that midday meals and other school nutrition measures may lead to parents reallocating scarce resources away from children at home (Kristjansson et al, 2006). If reallocation occurs, this is likely to be because there are other important unmet needs (for example, nutrition needs of younger siblings). But such effects would also reduce the impact on the intended recipients, and so smaller effects would be observed for the targeted group. Drawing on evidence from 18 studies across low-, middle- and high-income countries covering school-age children, one review of school nutrition programmes examined physical health and other benefits. For low- and middle-income countries, that review identified benefits in school attendance and increases in maths test scores. Results also pointed towards improved child weight and height, for younger children in particular, although the gains were small (Kristjansson et al, 2006). Positive impacts on children's growth have also been found in a Young Lives study that linked the Indian Midday Meal Scheme to physical recovery of young children during periods of drought (Singh et al, 2013).

Access to school

During the Millennium Development Goal period, there was an emphasis on eliminating school fees to boost school access. Evidence from Kenya, Malawi and Uganda links that change to increased enrolment (Morgan et al, 2012, p 25). One review of diverse school measures examined 73 studies and reported average impacts in the order of a 9% increase in student enrolment, a 7–8% increase in attendance, a 2–3% decrease in early school departure, and a 6–7% improvement in grade progression (Petrosino et al, 2016, pp 41–2). The largest impacts on access were associated with new infrastructure (such as building new schools or improving road access to schools). Four further categories – healthcare and nutrition, economic interventions (including cash transfers), educational practice/programmes, and information and training – were shown to have smaller effects of similar sizes (Petrosino et al, 2016, p 40). Another review identified similar factors, also finding evidence for effects of midday meals in schools and of low-cost private schools. However, this review found that cash transfers were associated with the largest and most consistent effects across most contexts (Snilstveit et al, 2015).

Quality of education

Studies tend to employ rather narrow indicators of quality – for example, ability in reading and/or maths – to understand learning. In addition, use of different indicators makes it challenging to compare results across studies (see Evans and Popova, 2015). Nevertheless, an examination of six systematic reviews suggested common messages (Evans and Popova, 2015). The largest positive effects were identified from pedagogical interventions, such as computer-based learning and measures that match teaching to children's learning levels, one caveat being that technology may be reliant on access to electricity. The second largest set of effects related to teacher training, with the review arguing that to produce effects interventions had to be long term (see also Orr et al, 2013). The third area related to teacher incentives, such as contract reform, pointing to accountability and motivation as important. The evidence for incentives comes predominantly from India and Kenya, weakening the transferability of those messages. The review also identified information provision (presumably to parents and children) about school quality and returns from education, and infrastructure investments in desks and chairs, as important for learning. The same review also considered evidence on interventions not found to be effective. Standalone measures such as 'one laptop per child' were found to be ineffective without training. There was limited evidence for the effectiveness of health measures, such as nutrition supplementation, deworming and cost reduction – for example, grants or fee reductions – for learning, although the authors recognise that such measures may be needed to improve attendance as noted earlier (Evans and Popova, 2015, pp 11-16).

More recent systematic reviews are consistent in highlighting the importance of pedagogic reforms, teacher training and accountability. One study identifies the importance of 'participatory and community management interventions' in engaging communities and overcoming harmful norms (Masino and Nino-Zarazua, 2015). These community interventions were compared with top-down, government-led initiatives, such as allocating poor children to better-performing schools. While the benefits of good school management and community norms were discussed, the results of specific interventions were mixed, suggesting that reforms such as decentralisation of powers would not automatically improve results (Masino and Nino-Zarazua, 2015, pp 11-12). Community engagement may encourage accountability to children and families, leading to more regular teacher attendance at school (Guerrero et al, 2012). A third review reinforced the conclusion that pedagogic reforms are central to improving learning, and identified the role of merit-based scholarships (for example, a cash grant to cover school fees and other costs), school nutrition, extra time in school, and remedial education (Snilstveit et al, 2015, p IV). School-related physical and sexual violence and bullying are not widely covered by reviews focusing on learning, which is a concern given that there is good reason to suppose that prevalence is high and these experiences can have particularly (often gendered) detrimental consequences for learning (Parkes et al, 2016). Violent school environments are therefore not simply a serious threat to wellbeing, but likely also to undermine school engagement, and as such ought to be considered as part of school quality. Efforts to reduce violence against children are likely to be most effective when nested within existing national strategies (Know Violence in Childhood, 2017). Greater effort to reduce violence at school could therefore have wider societal benefits.

Private schools

Private schools are increasing in number in many areas, including South Asia and sub-Saharan Africa (Morgan et al, 2012, p 23). Recognising the scale of the education crisis, many are interested in how the private sector might be used to raise delivery quality. Options to achieve this with equity include private delivery of education, publicly funded vouchers, and other measures to extend access to private schools. These very different options raise similar core questions around how to harness the private sector towards public objectives, while avoiding making gains for children in private schools at the expense of children in government schools.

Systematic review evidence on the effects of vouchers is based on a limited number of initiatives, so should be read with caution. One review identified studies from three countries (Morgan, et al, 2013). Evidence from Chile was from a large, well-established, scheme that provides a flat-rate voucher for school enrolment in either private or public schools. The scheme increased inequality in access to schools. A scheme in Colombia involved a voucher lottery, which could be used to cover some of the cost of secondary school places. This was directed at poorer communities and facilitated access to 'lower tier' private schools (that is, schools willing to accept vouchers). Positive results were found among lottery winners for years of schooling, grade completion and test scores (especially for girls), as well as reduced rates of marriage and cohabitation. Evidence from Pakistan drew on an assessment of a foundation-funded scheme aimed at educating girls in new private primary schools. A large increase in girls' enrolment was seen (and there was some increase in boys' enrolment too, likely due to greater overall capacity). No indication was given as to the effects of variation in quality. The review notes that to account fully for costs and benefits would require an assessment of the overall impact, including on children in government schools (potentially affected by greater social sorting; Morgan, et al, 2013, p 17).

There is a recent prominent example, in Liberia, of a more radical experiment to improve quality by outsourcing delivery of schools to the private sector (Romero et al, 2017). An evaluation after one year noted that children in the private schools had done better than those in the public schools, but questioned if these gains could be maintained at scale without changes in the model. There were concerns that private schools had 'pushed' some students and underperforming teachers into public schools. Gains in the private schools were in part at the cost of schools in the public system. None of that rules out the role of the private sector in delivering education, but as with provision of vouchers it does indicate that private delivery requires significant care and oversight and state regulation if it is to be consistent with equity goals.

Conclusion

Middle childhood is located between the rapid changes of early childhood and adolescence. There seems to be a longer window than previously thought during which changes in children's physical growth occur, and where improvements occur they are linked to important cognitive gains. The evidence from systematic reviews points to the importance of measures such as social protection, which has been shown to increase livelihood security. And with near-universal access to school during middle childhood, midday meals and other nutrition programmes in schools may also help support children's growth.

School is the dominant institution during middle childhood. Despite access gains, improvements in learning are far less evident, this now having become a central policy concern, as reflected in the SDGs. Many national school systems vary widely in the quality of education that they provide, exacerbating disparities due to household and community circumstances, and this indicates a need also for far greater consideration of equity. The focus on strengthened education and learning quality is especially important for the early grades, given that early performance in key areas such as literacy and numeracy lays the foundation for later educational performance. Of the Young Lives countries, Vietnam provides both efficiency and comparative equity in the education system. It is a model from which other countries can learn. School environments, especially sanitation and safety, have received less attention than they merit, yet are not only crucial to children's wellbeing, but also part of what makes a school effective for attendance and learning. Reviews suggest that measures such as curricular reform and better-trained and supported teachers will make an important difference to levels of learning achieved, with greater focus also required on improved infrastructure and less harsh disciplinary practices. Many children begin working during middle childhood and this can detract from their education. This highlights another important contribution for sustained support to household livelihoods through social protection, which can increase access to schools by reducing household reliance on children's work.

Notes

[1]   This does not mean that the velocity of gain for severely stunted children is less. The chance of being measured as recovered (that is, moving across the WHO threshold) combines the absolute HAZ gain and the HAZ starting point. By implication, the same absolute gain would be less likely to show

a severely stunted child as recovered, as against a moderately stunted child. We conclude that all children have some chance of recovery.

[2]   How boys and girls experience schools and learning is discussed in Chapter Six on adolescence, since this is when differences by gender become more notable (Singh and Krutikova, 2017).

[3]   This is because the time-use data are for a school day. Time use during the weekends and school holidays is clearly very different and so this may underestimate care activities and work.

[4]   Young Lives evidence on education is discussed by Rossiter and colleagues (2018), who make the case that basic skills are a civil right and that the failure of school systems to support children in attaining these skills is undermining children's participation in society.

[5]   The underlying value added analysis calculates the average differences between learning levels measured at the start and the end of the year.

SIX

Adolescence and youth: A time of responsibility and transformation

This chapter focuses on adolescence and youth, an extraordinarily dynamic period between the middle childhood years and young adulthood. In the Young Lives data, adolescence corresponds to the phase between the second and fourth survey rounds for the Older Cohort (12, 15 and 19 years) and the fourth and fifth rounds for the Younger Cohort (12 and 15 years). Adolescence is increasingly accepted as a particularly sensitive phase of human development, characterised by significant changes in the brain and body. Much is made of the heightened brain plasticity and emotional responsiveness during this period, wherein learning and adaptation are accelerated. This is the primary rationale for viewing adolescence as a second critical window for policy interventions to build on investments in early life and boost later chances. Yet these processes of change occur at a time when regulatory systems are still developing. So, while plasticity is taken to provide an opportunity to shape constructive values, attitudes and behaviours, immature self-regulation is regarded as a cause for concern, through its association with risk-taking activities that threaten healthy development.

These countervailing trends provide the rationale for numerous policies and interventions intended to promote positive development, spurred by the idea that many social orientations tend to crystalise during adolescence, laying down lifelong patterns. Similarly, there has been considerable policy momentum around adolescent sexual and reproductive health, community engagement and labour market readiness, and adolescents are also touched by many of the Sustainable Development Goals (SDGs), particularly SDG 4 on quality education and SDG 8 on decent work and economic growth. But recent initiatives such as the Lancet Commission on Adolescent Health and Wellbeing clarify that policy has neglected certain important aspects of adolescent health, as addressed in SDG 3. There are also significant evidence gaps, insofar as the vast bulk of research on adolescents is undertaken in high-income countries while the great majority in this age group live in low- and middle-income countries (LMICs). Similarly, while data disaggregation, as provided for in the SDGs, is a start, adolescents are not centre stage in any of the SDGs. In many contexts, adolescent girls continue to encounter the most significant challenges, reinforcing the importance of gender equity and girls' and women's empowerment, as specified in SDG 5 (UN Women, 2015).

As evidenced by Young Lives longitudinal findings, the current adolescent generation experiences better circumstances than that of their parents. Education has been central to this development and is seen as broadening horizons and fulfilling hopes for social advancement, so much so that young people increasingly seek to delay the age at which they enter work and start a family to concentrate on their studies. These positive trends notwithstanding, large proportions of young people in LMICs (particularly older adolescents) struggle to complete their education and many young people continue to see life chances undermined by extreme poverty, service shortfalls and other stressors. Poorer adolescents often face competing expectations and responsibilities, commonly juggling education with work and care roles. Meanwhile, decent work remains extremely scarce, with large numbers of young people working in irregular, low-paid jobs (Naafs and Skelton, 2018).

This chapter examines the development, experiences and perspectives of adolescents and youth, and in doing so explores how young people feel and respond to some of these challenges. The chapter reveals adolescence to be a key developmental milestone in the life course, when the effects of a multitude of developmental interactions from early and middle childhood begin to consolidate in increasingly mature cognitive, emotional and social functions (Masten and Cicchetti, 2010). It is a time of social transformation, associated with growing degrees of responsibility and gender differentiation, and for many, also with expanded social horizons. While many or most of the threats to young people's wellbeing and development originate in circumstances that are apparent even before birth, some arise during adolescence, further driving negative developmental cascades.

Nutrition and growth patterns during adolescence

Under favourable conditions, positive developmental momentum in physical growth, initiated in early life and consolidated in middle childhood, finds its strongest expression during adolescence. Positive developmental cascades may manifest across multiple areas of life, including the smooth progression through school, expansion of social networks, and enhancement of self-confidence. Examination of the middle-childhood predictors of adolescent functioning and wellbeing highlights how the interaction between different domains of development shapes these processes with cumulative effect, such that some adolescents become progressively more disadvantaged while others see their gains increase. Thus, for example, lower height-for-age among eight-year-olds is associated with lower learning levels at age 12 in all four countries, and height at age 12 is predictive of learning at age 15 in three countries.

To emphasise the rising momentum of negative developmental cascades through impaired growth in adolescence is not to deny the continuing possibility of remediation even in this late phase. As noted, Young Lives has considerable evidence that growth recovery – as well as faltering – and associated developmental change stretches up to at least age 15 (Fink and Rockers, 2014; Duc and Tam, 2015; Benny et al, 2017). Rates of recovery and faltering may vary between boys and girls. For instance, among the Older Cohort in United Andhra Pradesh, faltering in growth between ages 8 and 19 is far more likely among girls than boys (Himaz, 2018). In terms of the interactions between growth and wider wellbeing and resilience, becoming stunted as an adolescent is strongly correlated with reporting poorer relationships with peers compared with those never stunted, possibly due to bullying. There is also a significant correlation between stunting among adolescent girls and reduced height and weight in their offspring, as compared with the offspring of girls whose physical development was normal. This applies even when the young mothers were not stunted at age 8 or had recovered their growth by age 19 (Himaz, 2018). In other words, the persistence of negative developmental cascades through adolescence greatly increases the likelihood of inter-generational transmission of disadvantage, this being a motive for focusing investment on the development and wellbeing of adolescent girls.

One of the most significant risk factors for retarded growth is low birthweight. Young Lives data indicate that children who had low birthweights tended to have low pre-pubertal height and BMI. In United Andhra Pradesh, Peru and Vietnam, girls who had low birthweight were likely to have younger menarcheal ages. It may be the case that they are shorter at puberty simply because they have had fewer years in which to grow (Benny et al, 2018). Across all countries, later puberty in girls is linked with accelerated growth and greater height between 15 and 19 years of age (Benny et al, 2017). Growth recovery in girls between 15 and 19 years may be explained not simply by later puberty, but by increased dietary diversity. This suggests that recuperation in growth in adolescence can be promoted by nutritional interventions. However, there is a need to build a stronger evidence base through new analysis of existing data, and testing of interventions for adolescents.

Young Lives findings point to other risks – overweight and obesity – that have their roots in earlier childhood phases but become more prevalent during adolescence.[1] In the Young Lives sample, young people in Peru are the most affected, although rates have also grown noticeably among adolescents in Vietnam and United Andhra Pradesh. Figure 6.1 shows that around a third of the Older Cohort in Peru was overweight by age 22. Age 15 appears to be the tipping point when prevalence begins to rise fast, with females, and those who are better off and living in urban areas, the most affected. Girls who gained weight faster up to age 8 had a higher chance of early puberty. This is a concern since earlier puberty has been shown to bring greater risk of certain cancers, lifelong overweight and obesity, and lower linear growth (Aurino et al, 2017).

Peru is an upper middle-income country and its population is increasingly urban. Contributory factors in overweight and obesity include more sedentary lifestyles. Furthermore, Young Lives has also found that rising consumption of sugar, processed and high-energy foods, especially animal proteins, which is particularly common in urban areas, plays a part (Humphries et al, 2014; Benny et al, 2018).

Figure 6.1: Percentage of overweight children and young people (12-22 years), Peru

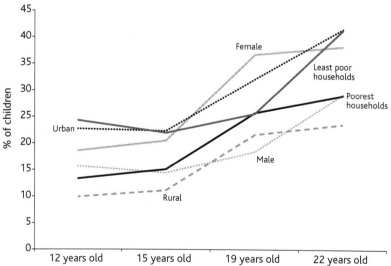

Moreover, and particularly worryingly, rates of overweight and obesity in adolescence are higher in the Younger Cohort than they are in the Older Cohort, indicating a rapid escalation, with serious risks for long-term health. At age 15, one in four (25%) of the Younger Cohort in Peru was overweight or obese as opposed to fewer than one in five (17%) of the Older Cohort. These findings illustrate the rapid shift in the malnutrition challenge in LMICs over recent decades, in which a sizeable proportion of adolescents experience the adverse consequences of exposure to obesogenic modern environments, namely low-quality diets and insufficient physical activity. The growing rates of obesity pose a huge threat to health in middle-income countries, specifically with respect to non-communicable diseases, the risks being highest for those who present with this condition early in life. What is also notable, in that context, is evidence that mothers tended to underestimate the weight of children who were overweight (Carrillo-Larco et al, 2017) suggesting perhaps a lack of recognition of this growing public health concern.

Education remains crucial to skills development during adolescence

Due to the recent expansion of secondary education – combined with policies making education compulsory up to a later age – school has become the predominant institutional context for learning during adolescence. By the same token, school performance and outcomes can be decisive in shaping adolescent transitions into adulthood. In all the Young Lives countries, school attendance among the Older Cohort was both relatively high and consistent through all ages up to around 14-15 years (Espinoza-Revollo and Porter, 2018). Inter-cohort comparison reveals further improvements in education access among this age group even in the relatively short period of seven years between the cohorts. However, more disadvantage is evident in Ethiopia than the other countries, not just because children in that country start school later, and spend less time in school and more time at work, but also because, beginning around mid-adolescence, many attend only intermittently and/or leave school early. Even so, by 2016, enrolment in the Younger Cohort in Ethiopia at age 15 was higher than in the Older Cohort at the same age (93% vs 90%). In United Andhra Pradesh 91% of 15-year-olds were enrolled in secondary schools, up from 78% in 2009. Significantly, enrolment increases in United Andhra Pradesh were particularly large for girls, Scheduled Tribes, Scheduled Castes and Backward Classes, groups that had previously lagged far behind.

Among other influences, enrolment increases reflect high ambitions. In the survey, young people and their caregivers were asked the stage, or number of years, of schooling aspired to and the majority indicated university. This evidence confirms that education is especially prized by rural populations as a means of ensuring that the young will be released from a life of poverty, hardship and struggle. A father in Peru reflected as follows: 'I ... walk in the fields with sandals. At least he will go with shoes if he gets a good head with education' (quoted in Crivello, 2011, p 404). Above all else, schooling is perceived as the most effective vehicle for escaping work in agriculture, which is regarded by young and old alike as an extremely arduous, low-status occupation offering poor returns. For girls, education has the additional value of being seen as improving marriage prospects, as Harika, in United Andhra Pradesh, put it:

> You get better jobs if you study and you have a better life and can marry an educated husband. If your husband is in agriculture, you have to go to the fields and work. If he is educated, you can be happy. We see our parents working and we feel that we do not want to be like them. They work in the fields and work hard every day. (Quoted in Boyden, 2013, p 585)

Educational ambitions do not stop at secondary schooling, since the majority of caregivers and adolescents report high hopes of going to university. Aspirations matter not only for the hopes they signal, but also because they influence education outcomes. These influences work through various mechanisms. For example, in United Andhra Pradesh it was found that, after controlling for a wide range of background and child characteristics, aspiring to one additional year of schooling was linked to an increase in the grade achieved at age 15 by 1.8 years on average (Serneels and Dercon, 2014). Similar effects were also found for results in mathematics and verbal tests. Aspirations matter less for grade attainment in children from wealthier backgrounds and with better-educated mothers. In Ethiopia, while aspirations remain high, they adjust through adolescence to realities imposed by economic constraints (Favara, 2016). Thus, this evidence does not tell us that low aspirations explain low engagement with education, since realising ambitions rests on both hopes and opportunities. So, for example, while high parental aspirations are likely to be associated with caregivers investing more in education, such as by paying for private tuition, this also depends on household resources. In Vietnam, parents in urban areas are better able to support young people's learning than are those in rural areas by sparing them from household chores, allowing them to concentrate on their studies (Huong, 2011).

The growing commitment to education is reflected in changes in adolescents' time use in the period 2006 to 2016, though increasing household wealth may also be a factor here. Inter-cohort comparison shows that the pressures on 15-year-olds to work fell in the Younger Cohort, while time spent at school rose. United Andhra Pradesh saw the largest change, ending up with the highest rate of school attendance and lowest work participation. Sarada, a young woman from Poompuhar, exemplifies young people's strong belief in the value of education, which in her case involved combatting firmly embedded gender norms (Crivello and Morrow, forthcoming, p 14). Sarada comes from a low-caste community and has been disabled since birth so cannot walk long distances. She has faced many hardships, including recurrent bullying by her peers. Sarada's family was in debt and she worked to help pay for her school transport, her sister's marriage and food. And when she was 13 the family's home collapsed following heavy rains. Despite these challenges, Sarada remained at school with the support of a local self-help group and a disability association and when her parents urged her to leave she managed to persuade a labour inspector to compel her parents to allow her to remain. By age 22, she had become a teacher and was registered at university.

Mesih, from rural Tigray in Ethiopia, shows similar ambitions (Young Lives, 2016). He is one of five children and his family is poor. Due to his livestock herding responsibilities, he started school late, at age 9. He continued to work throughout his time at school, cleaning sheep's wool, and collecting firewood and water. His work commitments and sickness meant that he frequently missed school, so it was not simply that he needed to catch up having started late, but he began to fall progressively behind. By age 14, he was only in fourth grade, when some of his friends had reached eighth grade. Nonetheless, Mesih was very determined and studied hard. Sometimes ranked top in his year, his family rewarded him with new clothes and school supplies and he was much encouraged. However, his circumstances did not improve. When he was 18, his father died and his community was affected by serious drought. Mesih moved to town to live with his sister. At 22, he is still studying and wants to be an entrepreneur. Mesih's case highlights the centrality of aspirations in shaping effort, but the contextual supports for their realisation, such as quality education and provision for homework, are often lacking.

The Older Cohort had reached age 22 years by the fifth survey round, this making it possible to see how many had achieved their ambition of continuing through tertiary education. Table 6.1 indicates disparities by gender and economic status in access to tertiary education and vocational training. In all four countries, poorer young people are consistently much less likely to have attended either university or vocational and technical levels of education. Again, differences between young men and young women are nationally specific. Men were more likely to have received both vocational and university education in United Andhra Pradesh, while in Vietnam women were more likely to have attended university.

Table 6.1: Highest education level achieved, or in progress, at age 22 (%)

	Ethiopia		India (UAP)		Peru		Vietnam	
	University	Vocational/ technical	University	Vocational/ technical	University	Vocational/ technical	University	Vocational/ technical
Women	16	19	30	6	26	27	37	21
Men	15	12	37	10	25	25	26	23
Bottom wealth tercile	7	6	22	7	13	24	15	10
Top wealth tercile	32	24	48	9	50	26	47	32
Average	15	15	34	8	26	26	31	22

Source: Favara et al (2018)

Education systems can push adolescents out of school

The intensive engagement with education during adolescence suggests that any limitations to school success are not due to low adolescent and parental ambition. Indeed, many young people remain hopeful that education will bring them high returns even in the face of grade repetition and poor exam performance. Nonetheless, by mid-adolescence, failings in school quality – combined often with the opportunity costs of attendance and rising doubts about the relevance of continued education for jobs – increasingly undermine school attendance and retention. While education policy often focuses on reforming pedagogy and curricula, Young Lives evidence establishes the need for far greater attention, in addition, to school environments, as noted in Chapter Five. Corporal punishment, bullying, and poor-quality infrastructure also affect progress and retention, as much as wellbeing.

Some challenges are specific to secondary and tertiary education. For example, in rural areas there tend to be fewer secondary school places than there are young people of secondary-school age, and the schools that do exist are generally of lower quality than in urban areas. Thus, unsurprisingly, education supply has become an important driver in rural-to-urban migration among adolescents, many of whom migrate on their own. Between a third (in Ethiopia) and a half (in United Andhra Pradesh) of the Older Cohort migrated within their countries through ages 15 to 19 years, and study was the chief motive across all four countries (Gavonel, 2017). Less-educated young people are more likely to migrate for work, whereas the better-educated are likely to migrate for university or training. In United Andhra Pradesh and Ethiopia, rural youth are most likely to migrate, in Peru and Vietnam, migration is more common among those in poorer households. Aspirations play a key role, especially for boys in United Andhra Pradesh and Vietnam (Gavonel, 2017). But young migrants can then find themselves torn between the desire to remain in education and the need to continue assisting their families. As a young teenager, Rajesh, from United Andhra Pradesh, wanted to be a doctor. He moved away from home to study in a hostel school. However, his health was poor and, facing economic difficulties, his family sought his help on the farm. By the age of 15 he had moved back home and had given up the idea of studying medicine (Boyden, 2013). Similarly, Huu, in Vietnam, stayed with an uncle in town so he could attend high school. But the uncle required him to work in his shop and so he fell increasingly behind with his studies. Eventually, when his brother enlisted in the military, Huu left school and returned home to support his mother and care for his sick father (Boyden, 2013).

Education quality shortcomings at secondary level are particularly evident in Ethiopia, United Andhra Pradesh and Peru. For example, the majority of the Younger Cohort in Peru were unable to solve several quite simple mathematical problems at age 15. Moreover, and in the same country, educational disparities that had arisen in early and middle childhood persisted into adolescence, with those who were poorer, from an ethnic minority, and living in a rural area continuing to be behind their peers. In Ethiopia, adolescents from the poorest households, those whose caregivers had little or no education, and those in rural areas, performed worse than urban children and those with more educated parents on tests of maths and vocabulary, and progressed more slowly through grades. By age 15, when they should have reached grade 7 or 8, they had typically only completed grade 5 or 6, with low school quality one of the contributory factors. While poor school quality is one probable reason for being over age for their grade, others include domestic responsibilities that impact time for study as discussed below (and in Chapter Seven), and which affect poor children far more than those who are better off.

As Chapter Five noted, Vietnam's education system is relatively more effective than those in the other Young Lives countries both in terms of quality and equity; strikingly, even those adolescents in Vietnam who leave school early are better educated than peers, many of whom remain at school, in the other three countries. Nevertheless, Vietnam's secondary education does not compensate fully for disadvantages associated with family background, as ethnicity and caregivers' education remain a major influence on school grades and performance in maths and vocabulary tests at age 15. Moreover, among those in the Younger Cohort whose caregivers had no schooling, enrolment declined substantially between ages 12 and 15, from 86% to 55%; while almost all (92%) of those whose caregivers had nine years of schooling or more were still enrolled at 15.

Although adolescents are generally at lower risk of corporal punishment in school than younger children (see Chapter Five), they still frequently report incidents of violence from their teachers. Peer bullying is also common. Poor children are more at risk in all four countries. They are susceptible to being disciplined by teachers for lacking the proper school materials or missing school for work, and bullying by peers because of their poverty. Rayma, from Poompuhar in United Andhra Pradesh, highlighted her struggle to balance agricultural work with school, and the punishments handed out for absences:

> Sometimes they [teachers] also beat us. Madam beats us more. She sometimes beats with stick. Everybody, all teachers, hold a stick whether they beat or not to discipline the students.... If we do not complete our homework, she beats. She scolds if homework is not done. She beats if homework is not done. She beats if [we are] not regular to school. (Quoted in Morrow and Singh, 2014, p 12)

In Vietnam, minority ethnic pupils are particularly susceptible to maltreatment. Y Thinh, a 16-year-old from the Cham H'roi ethnic group, recalled being mocked and punched by another boy for being 'an ethnic'. He maintained that bullying undermined his learning: 'I couldn't digest lessons. So I felt tired of learning' (quoted in Pells and Morrow, 2018, p 13). He eventually left school to work on his family's farm.

The interconnectedness of violence across life spaces emerges strongly, highlighting the complex interaction of stressors at micro, meso and macro levels. It is not uncommon for young people to be both bullied and punished at school, and then disciplined at home for getting into trouble at school. Secondary school may also present a more threatening environment for girls than primary school. In Peru, for example, boys often use physical aggression as a way of asserting masculine identities, while young women report bullying in the form of emotional violence. Susan, from Lima, said:

> Everything is different … you see, in primary school you have that warmth of being a girl with her back pack, nobody robs you, you can go calm, but in secondary school you have to take care of yourself because you are studying with older people, from fifth, fourth grade. (Quoted in Ames and Rojas, 2010, p 29)

Amina in Ethiopia described a similar experience:

> I do not like the behaviour of boys in the school, as they force girls to become their girlfriends. The teachers did the same as well. Last year, my homeroom teacher asked me to be his girlfriend. But when I refused, he reduced my results and told me that I had failed and I was going to repeat the grade. (Quoted in Pankhurst and Tiumelissan, 2013, p 23)

Longer journeys, at times unaccompanied, between home and secondary school can expose girls to the risk of sexual assault. In Ethiopia and United Andhra Pradesh, girls said they felt unsafe in school particularly due to a lack of gender-segregated toilets, which was associated with harassment from boys, particularly during menstruation. One 15-year-old girl in rural United Andhra Pradesh stated:

> We do not have bathrooms there.…. It is very difficult for us, particularly girls, and those who come from neighbouring villages. During the monthly cycles it is more difficult, so some girls don't come to school on those days. (Quoted in Pells and Morrow, 2018, p 13).

Unhospitable school environments and other systems shortcomings aside, many young people feel that the benefits of secondary education diminish with age, to the point where attendance drops significantly (Favara, 2016). This is especially true for poorer adolescents, those whose school performance is weak and those in communities where the links between education outcomes and labour market entry are tenuous. While there is broad gender parity in Peru, in Vietnam and Ethiopia school retention is a greater problem for boys than for girls, whereas girls experience the greater challenge in United Andhra Pradesh. Early departure by boys is due to a complex mix of rising demands and opportunities around paid work and increasing opportunity costs of school, as well as their poorer performance in school. Early school departure has important implications for future employment and in the case of girls raises the possibility of early marriage and parenthood.

The demands of education, work and care can be excessive

Not all of the competences required for adulthood can be learnt at school. In many contexts, adolescence is when the young are expected and seek to gain the skills necessary for contributing to the household, conserving strong familial bonds, and becoming productive adult members of society. Work is commonly understood as the most valuable setting for learning these kinds of skills. Moreover, household livelihoods are often reliant on all members contributing labour according to their ability. However, the concern to meet filial responsibilities does not diminish the enthusiasm for education, which may be as much about securing a better future for the family as it is about personal gain. In this sense, combining work and education during adolescence can be seen as fulfilling an implicit inter-generational contract. Work and education need therefore to be considered not as separate activities but in combination, with each having bearing on a young person's future job prospects as much as family welfare. Under these circumstances, adolescents' aspirations are often decidedly pro-social. By the same token, the centrality of adolescents' work contribution means that attributes in the young, such as empathy, diligence and cooperation, are highly appreciated. A mother in rural Ethiopia reasoned:

> If the parents are poor the child can support their parents, even the young ones.... They feel that they shouldn't sit while suffering with poverty. They want to help their

mothers and they go with their mothers. (Interview transcript)

In all four countries, adolescents report feeling pride in their ability to assist their families through work, and consider it a part of being a 'good child' (Morrow and Boyden, 2018). One boy in United Andhra Pradesh said: 'I felt very happy. I want to get a good name, still want to work hard and do better things' (quoted in Morrow and Boyden, 2018, p 29).

During adolescence especially, work also enables young people to gain a foothold in highly competitive labour markets and can be a backup if education fails to improve their prospects, or better jobs are not available. For example, a 15-year-old boy in United Andhra Pradesh described his work as a form of insurance:

As it is, we are not sure of getting employment after completion of education.... So, we cannot depend on one source for employment alone. We have to take up studies and work simultaneously during holidays. (Quoted in Rolleston and James, 2011, p 11)

Similarly, a boy in Ethiopia explained:

My father said to me that you should know my work because it will help you in the future if you could not be successful in your education; he says that you can be a good farmer..... (Interview transcript)

The evidence that many young people combine multiple tasks, with some dipping in and out of school along the way, disproves the common policy assumption of a single, definitive transition from education to work. For many the work burdens are considerable. In 2006, a third of 15- to 17-year-olds in Young Lives Older Cohort households worked for more than six hours per day (Boyden et al, forthcoming a). However, by 2016, and for the Younger Cohort, this had fallen notably in Peru, Vietnam and particularly United Andhra Pradesh, though far less so in Ethiopia. In Peru and Vietnam, young people from minority ethnic groups work significantly more than those in the majority groups. Large numbers of 15-year-olds also report involvement in at least one hazardous activity, as indicated in Table 6.2. In United Andhra Pradesh and Peru, working in the hot sun or rain is the most common risk.

Table 6.2: Percentage of 15-year-olds engaged in hazardous activities

	Ethiopia		India (UAP)		Peru		Vietnam	
	Boys	Girls	Boys	Girls	Boys	Girls	Boys	Girls
Carrying heavy loads	34.4	29.0	45.7	21.5	20.8	12.8	19.2	9.8
Using dangerous tools	50.2	62.4	30.1	23.4	26.5	32.1	40.3	41.4
Handling chemicals	17.1	7.5	13.0	13.3	10.2	4.1	11.0	12.0
Working under the hot sun or in the rain	43.9	31.0	52.3	30.6	27.7	17.2	28.1	18.6
Working with or close to animals	43.3	28.0	18.1	3.7	19.8	16.6	17.8	12.6
Working with insufficient lighting	7.9	7.6	5.2	0.9	5.0	3.5	2.7	1.2
Working in very noisy environment	6.4	5.6	7.0	2.5	7.9	5.2	8.5	8.3
Working with fumes, gases, dust	23.6	23.9	31.0	29.3	8.4	6.1	7.0	5.4
Being close to moving vehicles or driving	8.6	6.2	8.3	2.4	4.5	1.8	8.2	4.3
Working in a smelly and/or dirty environment	8.3	7.0	17.4	10.8	3.8	2.4	10.5	9.1
Working in heights	11.6	7.3	4.4	1.0	3.6	0.7	4.6	0.8
Working in a risky or unsafe environment[a]	4.9	3.9	–	–	–	–	–	–
Affected children	956	854	775	676	853	826	718	652

Notes: The specific question asked is: 'Think about any paid or unpaid work you do, or any chores you do around the house. Do any of these activities involve any of the following things [list as per column one]?'

[a] Work activities in unsafe environments are specified as those involving any of the following: use of machetes, knifes, scythe or fertilisers, pesticides, solvents or paints; and working in bars, or on the street.

Source: Boyden et al (forthcoming)

Age 14-15 is a key transition point, from lower secondary education in Ethiopia and United Andhra Pradesh, and to upper secondary education in Peru and Vietnam, and often when adolescents leave school. Nevertheless, many continue their education alongside work. As the competing demands of education, work and care mount up, so adolescents contend with growing and increasingly conflicting pressures. Beyond the challenge of sustaining school attendance in contexts of poor quality and progress, excessive chores and work in middle adolescence can put school learning at risk, as shown in Chapter Seven. Defar, from Ethiopia, highlighted the difficulty of combining school and work. He had only reached grade 4 in school by age 17. His slow progress was partly due to intermittent attendance, which he attributed to family poverty and the demands of work:

> Last September when I asked my parents to send me to school, they said that they do not have the economic power, so then I left. I started working because I was hungry ... they were not able to provide me with exercise books ... I realized that my family was very poor. (Interview transcript)

Defar would help his father collect and sell stones in town, although the work was hard and the pay low. This reality is very different from the image conveyed in many policy and research debates, in which adolescence is often regarded as a time of irresponsible experimentation and risk taking.

Some occupations have flexible schedules, so that the combination of school and work is less onerous, while others make schooling impossible (Tafere and Pankhurst, 2015). The fall-off in school attendance is especially apparent among adolescent boys in Ethiopia and Vietnam, as is the increase in the time they spend working. In Ethiopia, one reason is a recent rise in off-farm employment in some rural areas, which is frequently full-time and so precludes schooling (Boyden et al, 2016). Aspirations also decline at this point as everyday realities begin to undermine hopes for a better future (Favara, 2016).

Leaving school early through pressure of work is not at all straightforward and can cause difficulties between adolescents and their parents; having frequently made significant sacrifices to enable their children to attend, including selling property and getting into debt, some parents are extremely disappointed – even angry. Atilio, from Andahuaylas in Peru, left school early and moved to Lima to work in the market (Boyden, 2013). His mother worries that he has compromised his chances by not completing secondary school, and that without qualifications he will be forced to work in agriculture, stating that 'all his life he will suffer in the fields' (interview transcript). She argued that he had broken an explicit agreement between them: 'He said to me, "I'm not going to be like everyone else, I am going to study" ... he told me that he would study perhaps to be an engineer' (interview transcript). She therefore perceives that her sacrifice and investment in his secondary school education has been wasted: '[It seems] I put him [in secondary school] just for the sake of it' (interview transcript). Atilio, though, is adamant that he will do far better by working in Lima. Then again, many other adolescents in his situation express deep anxiety about letting their families down, and about the stigma of school failure, and some are resentful about giving up their education for the sake of the family.

As young people age, time spent in education falls and time at work increases, as can be seen in Figure 6.2. By age 19, between six and eight out of every 10 young people (United Andhra Pradesh and Vietnam) reported being in some form of work, although often they were still studying, so the pressures had not necessarily lessened. By

Figure 6.2: Percentage of young people aged 19 and 22 working and studying

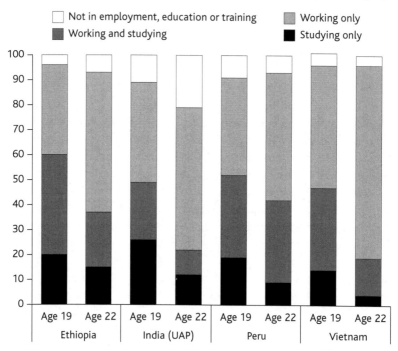

Source: Favara et al (2018)

22 years of age, however, participation in work had increased further in all countries, and between half (Peru) and three quarters (Vietnam) were working only. Men had higher employment rates at both ages, but the gap narrowed with age, as more women were working at 22 than at 19. Conversely, nearly two in five young people in Ethiopia and Peru, and one in five in United Andhra Pradesh and Vietnam, were still engaged in some form of study, often doing so alongside work. In some contexts (for example, Peru), this reflects a rise in access to tertiary education, while in others (such as Ethiopia) many young people are simply behind the education level expected for their age. A much smaller minority reported not being in employment, education or training, a category that included many young women who were married, many of whom were also mothers.

Unsurprisingly, the poorest young people tended to cease education and begin working at younger ages (Favara et al, 2018). Unemployment was comparatively rare, but underemployment perhaps higher. Using employment benefits or contracts of employment as proxies for quality, the quality of jobs was often low. Only one in 20 (6%) of those in waged work in United Andhra Pradesh reported having a contract of employment, while the figures for Ethiopia were 23%, and for Peru 34%, with quality seemingly quite a bit higher in Vietnam, at 62% (Favara et al, 2018). Young waged workers in Vietnam were much more likely to have a written contract and better access to employment benefits – for example, social insurance – than in the other countries.

Gender is a defining aspect of adolescent experience

In many LMICs, adolescence involves major social transitions. Gender becomes more prominent in shaping expectations, roles and conduct, giving rise to significant adjustments at school, in work, friendships and virtually all other aspects of life. Boys and girls commonly experience very different opportunities and constraints, so that their trajectories become increasingly divergent as they age. In policy it is usually held that these processes entail systematic gender discrimination, whereby girls and women are consistently disadvantaged when compared with boys and men. It is assumed that young males are channelled largely into productive roles and young females into reproductive roles, with young men's horizons widening and young women's narrowing. To a degree, Young Lives evidence corroborates this understanding. For example, girls living in households containing young children report considerably more time caring for others than do boys living in similar households, and housework and caring for ill or ageing family members is one of the main reasons girls stop attending school (Crivello and Espinoza-Revollo, 2018, p 148). Adolescent girls are also far more likely to cohabit, marry and/or become a parent than are adolescent boys, while more boys generally enter employment than girls, as noted. However, the findings around gender vary across contexts and are quite subtle and complex, and the patterns change with age. In particular, adolescent boys are not necessarily better off than their female peers in all areas of life, although girls are systematically disadvantaged in United Andhra Pradesh (Dercon and Singh 2013).

Some complexities of gender during adolescence can be seen in Figure 6.3, which depicts boys' and girls' time use in rural Ethiopia across various activities and ages. Overall, boys' workloads rise with age, and are more likely to involve herding and cultivation, while girls are more likely to assume domestic chores and care roles, although these decline with age. While tasks clearly do become more gendered with age, and are broadly separated into stereotypical roles, the division of labour is not a simple binary, insofar as both boys and girls often undertake tasks commonly associated with the opposite gender. For example, the degree of paid work undertaken by girls is perhaps surprising. Typical gender roles may even be reversed in adolescence due to household circumstances, and to the birth order, age or gender composition of the sibling group (Heissler and Porter, 2013).

Gender differences are also evident in learning outcomes, although the patterns are complex and diverge by country. This is shown in Figure 6.4, which gives scores on quantitative tests at ages 5 through 19 years. Points above the line indicate where boys are doing better

Figure 6.3: Daily tasks and gender in rural Ethiopia

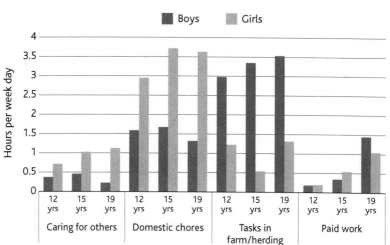

Figure 6.4: Differences in quantitative test score performance between boys and girls (standard deviation units)

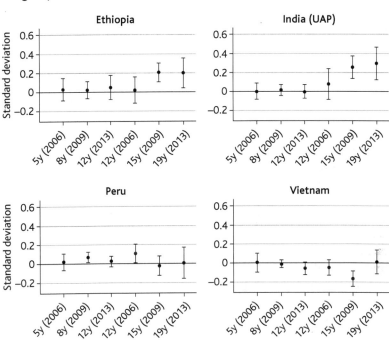

Source: Singh and Krutikova (2017, Figure 2)

than girls, and points below the line indicate where girls are doing better. Where the confidence intervals overlap the line, there is no significant difference found between boys and girls (Singh and Krutikova, 2017). Again, the figure shows that these disparities are not very strong in middle childhood, but in United Andhra Pradesh and Ethiopia a pro-boy advantage emerges very clearly in mid-adolescence, whereas in Peru there is no discernible disparity and in Vietnam girls perform better than boys at 15.

Despite overall gains in girls' enrolment in United Andhra Pradesh, school retention becomes more challenging as young women progress through adolescence. Secondary schools in that country often fail to accommodate the needs of girls; poor sanitary provision, for example, is humiliating for girls and undermines beliefs concerning the centrality of female modesty. The geographic dispersal of secondary schools also presents particular safety and social risks for girls, as noted. But gender preferences concerning options for girls' futures are another determining factor. In this context, girls are generally expected to marry out of the family and contribute to their husbands' households, and parents thus have little incentive to support their continued education (Dercon and Singh, 2013). The payment of dowry by the bride's family to the groom's family is another factor, since the cost of dowry rises as a girl grows older and becomes more educated; this also exerts a downward pressure on the age at which girls marry, as Prema explained:

> You see, we have to give more dowry as my age and qualifications increase. My parents have to search for a boy having higher qualifications and age. We came across this alliance who are also related to us. My elder brother told us about this alliance. And that's how I got married. (Quoted in Crivello et al, 2018, p 34)

Reducing the pressure on girls to marry and become parents below age 18 is a major focus of gender policy globally. Although the age of marriage is inching upward in most countries, poverty remains one of the key drivers of child marriage and the age gap between the poorest girls and their wealthier peers is widening (Lenhardt and Shepherd, 2013). Changing prevalence in the Young Lives countries reflects these global trends, for example in Ethiopia (Pankhurst, 2014) and United Andhra Pradesh (Singh and Vennam, 2016). By age 19, between one seventh and one third of young women were married or cohabiting. The rates for young men are much lower, at between 1% in Ethiopia and 7% in Peru. Child marriage (marriage by 18) was most common in United Andhra Pradesh, where 28% of girls were married by this age and 13% were parents. A full 92% of those in United Andhra Pradesh who were married by age 19 were from rural areas and migration for marriage is particularly common in this context (Gavonel, 2017).

Aside from policy concerns about child/early marriage and cohabiting as a threat to young women's health, wellbeing and rights, there are also concerns about its association with early parenthood, which is another source of health and social risk – to both mother and child. Figure 6.5 tracks the age of parenthood among the Older Cohort by household wealth level, and shows that the rate of becoming a parent is higher among those from poorer backgrounds and accelerates through the late teen years.

Ensuring that young women continue to attend school and retain positive social networks is an important factor in delaying early marriage. In United Andhra Pradesh and Vietnam, whether a girl is still in school at age 15 is the strongest predictor of whether she will

Figure 6.5: Age of parenthood by household wealth

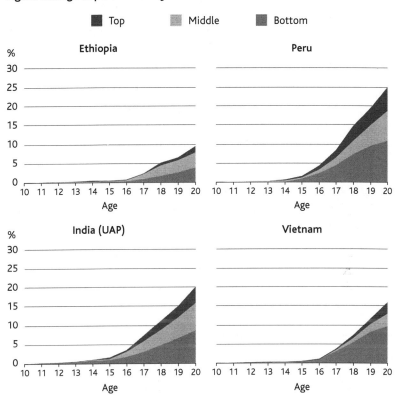

marry before age 19. In Peru and Ethiopia, there are strong correlations between the highest grade completed, school achievement and the incidence of early marriage or cohabitation (YMAPS [Young Marriage and Parenthood Study], 2018). In some contexts, encouraging families to allow their daughters to remain in school and delay marriage means addressing entrenched patriarchal values. A rise in the age of marriage and parenthood among girls in Vietnam seems to be linked to changing gender attitudes and to young people having a greater say in decisions affecting their futures (Zharkevich et al, 2016). The policy challenge is greater in contexts where patriarchal norms are bolstered by powerful economic incentives. In Ethiopia, most marriages are arranged by the couples' families, and form part of a wider economic transaction between their kin focused on the payment of bride price (Boyden et al, 2012). Marriages arranged early secure these transactions, providing strong economic and social incentives, especially in poor communities. Seen as transitioning girls into adulthood, providing them and their offspring with social, physical and material security, and preventing them from engaging in unprotected pre-marital sex, and incurring the risk of sexually transmitted infections, pregnancy out of marriage, and related stigma, early marriage is also regarded as protective. Whether unions are arranged by the family is considered to be of greater importance than the age of marriage, since arranged marriages enjoy far greater social recognition and family support.

In many contexts, marriage is, in effect, an alternative to paid employment for young females (Jensen and Thornton, 2003). Haymanot, in Ethiopia, left school early to help support the family when her mother became ill. She took a job in a stone-crushing plant, but found the work difficult, so married at age 16:

> I was happy to marry; nobody forced me to.… I am happy with my marriage because it was arranged by my parents [mother]. It also relieved me of the heavy work which I had to do. I had no plan to marry early. But when I left school and had such a tough job, I wanted to marry and take rest. (Quoted in Pankhurst, 2014, p 4)

Although Haymanot had welcomed marriage, she and her husband separated soon after the birth of their child. Marriage also prevented her from continuing her education, since remaining at school under these circumstances is constrained by norms against mothers attending school, and by childcare needs.

Social networks are vital to resilience and coping in the face of adversity

Transitioning to secondary school, and engaging in work outside the domestic sphere and in other activities, often expands adolescents' social networks – again, with gender an important distinguishing factor. Despite different social norms in different contexts, the importance of social support and improving social capital in adolescence is evident in all four countries. Social networks may centre on members of the family, peers and/or neighbours, faith leaders and teachers, and entail anything from advice, encouragement and affect, to material assistance. In contexts where state services and safety nets are weak, resilience in the face of poverty and other adversities is often built through social support from peers, teachers and others (Crivello and Morrow, forthcoming). For example, kin may provide funds, cultural capital and information on how to navigate pathways to education and jobs. Following his parents' deaths, Afework, from Ethiopia, was only able to continue his education through the practical and financial assistance provided by a male cousin and his elder sister (Crivello and Morrow, forthcoming).

Supportive relationships may also allow adolescents to envision possible futures that are very different from those experienced by young people in the past, for example as when kin encourage the realisation of ambitions through migration. Money given to her by her family made it possible for Maria in Peru to move at the age of 12 to the town where her grandparents lived to access a better secondary school. Maria's parents were happy that their daughter did not have a long, potentially dangerous, school commute and that she was under the supervision of trusted family members. Later on, her aunt paid for her to attend nursing school. More than half of young migrants in United Andhra Pradesh, Peru and Vietnam receive remittances from their caregivers, and in Ethiopia migrants are more likely to receive remittances (46%) than transfer funds to their natal household (17%) (Gavonel, 2017). That said, even though migration is often facilitated by social networks, it can also reduce social support (Gavonel, 2017).

For some young people, teachers can be instrumental in safeguarding their hopes of a better future. A number of girls in Ethiopia explained that their teachers had persuaded their parents not to marry them off and to allow them to remain in school. Some teachers offer practical assistance when pupils fail exams or are absent from school due to illness or work. Lien, a young woman from rural Vietnam, experienced domestic violence while growing up. Her family is very poor and since her father was frequently away and rarely contributed to the household economically, she worked for pay, sewing bags. Her grandmother died on the day that she failed her high school entrance exam. The school's vice principal helped her register for additional courses to prepare her for resitting the exam. With the schools' backing and by managing to combine work with studies, she eventually passed and went on to study social work at university (Crivello and Morrow, forthcoming).

Though peers can cause much distress through bullying and exclusion from friendship groups, they can also be crucial to wellbeing during adolescence. Fifteen-year-old Nga, in Vietnam, highlighted how her friends, 'a few good children who had to quit school because of their family situation', relied on each other for emotional and financial support (Young Lives, 2015a, p 5). Likewise, Yaswanth, a 16-year-old boy in United Andhra Pradesh, explained that his friends give him school supplies, and helped him with his school fees and studying for exams. Despite his poverty, he shared his food with them and gave one some money to cover his examination fee (Morrow and Vennam, 2015). When Ranadeep, also from United Andhra Pradesh, missed school for work, his friends made sure he did not fall behind:

> I used to borrow the notes from my friends in the night, and used to say the answers when the teachers asked me. I used to ask my friends what they learned in school that day, and used to update myself … my friends helped me a lot…. Those who are good to us, we call them friends. (Quoted in Morrow and Vennam, 2015, p 157)

The importance of peer relationships can also be seen by their absence. For example, Y Mich, a boy from the Cham H'roi ethnic group in Vietnam, left school early despite having passed his exam and despite the disappointment expressed by his family. He reasoned that there were no other Cham H'roi students in his class, as his close friend confirmed: 'He confided once that he was sad as he could not talk to anyone in the class. He asked to move to another class but the head teacher did not allow that' (quoted in Le and Tran, 2013, p 17).

Gender norms permeate adolescents' social relationships in all Young Lives sites, whether among peer groups, at school, or in the family, and this requires that adolescents navigate shifting expectations around the conduct appropriate to boys and girls. With adolescence a time of increased gender segregation, these changes may lead girls especially to lose access to peer networks and other sources of support. In United Andhra Pradesh, girls' relationships with peers become far more restricted as they enter puberty. This is partially due to increased care responsibilities, but also to concerns that their honour will be compromised by entering public spaces unaccompanied, or through associating with young men (Young Lives, 2015a). Marriage is another factor in diminished access to support systems. Seble, a young woman from Ethiopia, recounted how she kept in contact with her mother when she was married at 16, despite tradition dictating that her mother should not set foot in her home until she had a baby (van der Gaag et al, 2012). However, she missed her friends, explaining that when a young woman is married,

> … it is not possible for her to meet people like she used to. Because she has a husband and she is in a marriage, she is not free to meet anyone at any time. I never wander around like I used to when I was young and single. I just stay at home and wait for him. (Quoted in Young Lives, 2015a, p 31).

Key findings from Young Lives on what matters in adolescence and youth

This chapter highlights the challenges and opportunities experienced by adolescents and youth as they transition towards young adulthood, pointing also to the cumulative effect of earlier circumstances in their lives and to the widely divergent pathways they follow. To summarise the key messages:

- Adolescence is a second window for intervention.
- Physical recovery and faltering continues through adolescence, with implications for wider development. Interventions to secure better physical development can support the health of young people and that of their future children.
- There is evidence of rising overweight across the adolescent years, increasing the risk of non-communicable diseases in later life.
- Adolescence is a time of growing social responsibilities – to work, and to care for family – alongside continued expectations for studying. The combined pressures of balancing education and work weigh most heavily on the poorest children and sometimes on girls.
- Education continues to dominate both hopes and time use during this phase of life, but as the opportunity costs of staying in school increase through adolescence, aspirations adapt and early departure is common.
- Migration from rural areas facilitates access to secondary education and better-quality schooling, but increases the pressures of combining study with family responsibilities.
- As at primary level, secondary schools can be unhospitable environments often characterised by violence, which serves to reduce children's participation.
- Gender differences become more important during adolescence, leading girls and boys to follow very different trajectories. But gender patterns are very complex and vary across contexts. In United Andhra Pradesh, girls are disadvantaged across multiple domains, but in Vietnam girls outperform boys in education.

Policy interventions in adolescence and youth

The SDGs address a range of concerns that are relevant for adolescents and youth, from child marriage and female genital mutilation to good-quality education and decent work, and there is a growing momentum in policies focused on adolescence. This is reflected in initiatives such as the Lancet Commission on Adolescent Health and Wellbeing (Patton et al, 2016). In its 2016 report, *Our future*, the Commission notes the 'triple dividend' accruing to investment in adolescents as improvements in health and wellbeing during adolescence itself, with lasting benefits also across the lifetime, and for the next generation (Patton et al, 2016). The upsurge in interest in adolescence is particularly relevant for LMICs, which have very large young populations. This demographic dividend offers a current boost to economic growth, but also requires education, jobs, and citizenship, in addition to health. In this sense, today's 'youth bulge' entails both opportunities and challenges for policy, national development and young people themselves. The following section outlines some specific policies and interventions that address a number of aspects of adolescents' and young people's lives.

Programming for adolescent health and wellbeing

The importance of nutrition. Since there are rapid physical changes and maturation during adolescence, nutrition is very important, and prioritising the nutrition of adolescent girls also benefits future offspring. A systematic review of nutrition interventions found positive results of supplementation for reducing anaemia, with supplementation for pregnant adolescents also improving subsequent child health (Salam et al, 2016a). The review highlighted important shortcomings of available evidence. Most studies focus on adolescent girls, while much less is known about adolescent boys, and there is a limited amount of data from LMICs and a wide (statistical) range of findings, indicating this is an under-researched area. There was also more evidence on the impact of school-based supplementation than for community interventions, which perhaps reinforces the significance of the school as a delivery platform, particularly for the early adolescence/lower secondary school phase.

The rise in overweight and obesity suggests a role for both market and regulatory reforms, and improvements in public understanding. Review evidence highlights the potential to use both health clinics (Nagle et al, 2013) and schools (Verstraeten et al, 2012) to promote healthy eating and exercise. One review argued that in schools multicomponent interventions (for example, promoting healthy eating and exercise through the curricula) were likely to be most effective, and highlighted how involving parents could improve effectiveness (Verstraeten et al, 2012). As with interventions to reduce under-nutrition, it was also noted that the success of particular platforms is dependent on populations having good access to key services (Nagle et al, 2013).

Continuing education

Secondary education. Many of the decisions made during later adolescence regarding time use and education relate to preparing for adult roles. Transitions to the labour market are chief among these. Insofar as secondary schooling has become the primary route to decent work, school retention during the adolescent years is vital. With rising enrolment rates at secondary level, schools also offer a platform for delivery of other interventions. But at present this is likely to be more effective during early adolescence (10-14) when enrolment rates are highest.

After mid-adolescence, it is increasingly likely that those who work and those from minority ethnic groups will cease to be enrolled in school, so retention is a major challenge. This implies attention to education quality and relevance to the adult world of work, equipping adolescents through academic or vocational instruction with skills that match local opportunities. It also involves fostering a school culture in which safety and respect for all students are assured and stigmatisation, corporal punishment and bullying are eliminated. Accepting that adolescents are likely to work and that combining work and school becomes harder as the demands increase with age, implies the need not just for active labour market policies and better workplace management, but also for changes in school systems, for example, flexible schedules, and re-enrolment and extra tuition for children who have dropped out. Community groups, sports clubs and other associations can positively engage young people who are out of school, providing opportunities to link to more formal education or training services (for example, Higginson et al, 2015).

Technical and vocational education and training (TVET). These interventions commonly involve classroom and/or on-the-job training. Reviews of studies in LMICs suggest a range of small positive impacts on employment, one review identifying the strongest effects on formal employment and monthly earnings, although there is some evidence that while young women's work hours were increased, young men's were not affected (Tripney et al, 2013, pp 11-12). This points to better effects for women, which is valuable since they are generally more marginalised in labour markets than men. Although arguing for the value of TVET, the reviewers note that the actual size of impacts is small and very different across studies, and that benefits to individuals may accrue in part by replacing others in the labour market rather than increasing the number of jobs (Tripney et al, 2013, p 37).

Job creation and entrepreneurship

An increasing number of countries face a jobs challenge, which is a clear area of concern for many governments. Alongside broader questions of whether economic growth is inclusive, there are a number of tangible areas of intervention.

Active labour market policies. The need to create decent jobs for young people in LMICs is critical and job creation is emphasised as a key global challenge in the 2013 World Development Report (The World Bank, 2012). The report identifies the private sector as the main source of jobs globally, but recognises the role of government in creating an enabling policy environment for the creation of good jobs by ensuring macro-economic stability, through regulation, targeted investment and other measures. Common approaches revolve around active labour market policies for training and supporting entrepreneurship. One review of these measures argued that policies that provide some level of skill development have a more significant impact for young people in LMICs than is often observed in high-income countries. The same review finds positive evidence for both training provision and for entrepreneurial support, suggesting that there is a need for both supply- and demand-side interventions to support employment (Kluve et al, 2017, p 141).

It is also important to develop far more effective policies for preventing harmful adolescent work. As indicated in Chapter Five, reducing family reliance on young people's labour through social protection and programmes that incentivise school attendance is one element in this approach that is already quite well established. But a great deal more needs to be done to understand and address hazardous and exploitative work. The International Labour Organization, in Convention number 182 (ILO, 1999), has established important norms proscribing young people's involvement in slavery or slavery-like practices, prostitution, pornography, illicit activities, such as the production and trafficking of drugs, and work that, by its nature or the circumstances in which it is carried out, is likely to harm their health, safety or morals. There is evidence that efforts to ban such work outright do not always yield the intended results, while through various programmes tailored to specific occupations and activities or specific groups of young workers – many of which involve close engagement with employers, families and communities – working hours can be reduced, education access increased and work conditions and terms of employment improved (Bourdillon et al, 2011). But there remain considerable challenges of scaling this work up, accessing some of the most vulnerable young workers, such as those in domestic service, and identifying which among a wide range of occupations and activities to prioritise.

Entrepreneurship. Reviews of programmes to improve entrepreneurship, such as vocational, business or financial training, suggest large effects on knowledge are possible from interventions, but one review did not find that this automatically results in more self-employment (Cho and Honorati, 2014). The authors argue that a combination of training and financing measures could be more successful in expanding entrepreneurship, with evidence that cash grants, rather than micro-credit allocations, are more successful (Cho and Honorati, 2014, p 124). Micro-finance initiatives aim to tackle poverty through access to financial products. Approaches include micro-credit (small-scale loans, predicated on supporting entrepreneurship, which in turn enables loan repayment), micro-savings and insurance. These measures are commonly directed towards women to improve their empowerment. The delivery of micro-credit has long been one of the most favoured approaches, although there is growing recognition that such measures do not provide an uncomplicated solution to poverty. In particular, one review finds little evidence that micro-credit is particularly effective at tackling poverty (Duvendack et al, 2011). Another review highlights concerns that credit may do harm in some circumstances, and advises lending to existing entrepreneurs, rather than assuming that all people can become entrepreneurs.

Micro-savings seem more likely to be effective than credit for young people in poverty (Stewart et al, 2010). One review considered self-help groups directed at women specifically, whose aim is to form groups explicitly intended to increase access to finance through collective saving and intergroup lending, often supplemented by other interventions such as training of members (Brody et al, 2016, p 91). Somewhat positive results in improving women's empowerment are reported, but the greatest impacts are in the outcomes of training, such as health education, and may be due to the effects of group organisation as much as financial inclusion. The review also warned that the poorest women are frequently excluded (Brody et al, 2016, p 91).

Sexual reproductive health, marriage, cohabitation and fertility

Marriage and fertility. Ensuring young people's sexual and reproductive health and preventing early/child marriage and fertility are major policy priorities globally. Young Lives evidence highlights that addressing these matters necessitates an understanding of the underlying norms, for example, the idea that high fertility proves male virility, or that marrying girls off early is protective in contexts of poverty and livelihood insecurity. Attention must also be given to school failings, such as poor learning progression, and unsafe and insanitary school environments. Measures that help girls to continue attending school, and cash transfers, are most clearly linked to reduced adolescent fertility (McQueston et al, 2012). Likewise, measures to keep girls in school for longer (for example, social protection and reducing school costs) can reduce rates of child marriage (and so also fertility) among girls, as can life-skills training. There is evidence from Ethiopia that cash payments delayed marriage in very early adolescence (10-14 years), but increased it in later adolescence (15-19 years; Kalamar et al, 2016). A second study confirmed the importance of both economic incentives and girls' empowerment, such as through life-skills training (Lee-Rife et al, 2012). While the wider benefits of measures to extend girls' schooling are emphasised, some studies also stress the importance of taking account of local norms in programme design, since they are key drivers of choice (McQueston et al, 2012, p 46; Wamoyi et al, 2014).

Due particularly to concerns about adolescent risk behaviours, much attention has been given to sexual and reproductive health in the adolescent years. The range of possible areas of intervention is demonstrated by one review that covered female genital mutilation/cutting (FGM/C) and intimate partner violence, alongside adolescent fertility (Salam et al, 2016b). For the reduction of adolescent fertility, the review identified the importance of health education, counselling and contraceptive availability, to both increase knowledge and contraceptive use. For FGM/C, the evidence points to community engagement and mobilisation, and to female empowerment, to promote awareness of the health consequences of FGM/C and facilitate mobilisation against the practice. Such findings reinforce evidence from Young Lives and elsewhere, that while legal approaches may be needed in some circumstances to outlaw particular practices, without interventions that address the underlying causes, these approaches may be both flawed and risk causing unintended adverse consequences.

Conclusion

Adolescence builds on the foundation that comes before but there are also particular dynamics that open up during this life phase. What is historically new is the increased number of years young people spend in schools, and this is intimately tied up with high hopes and aspirations. Hopes and aspirations are vital, but they are not enough. Without practical support young people are unlikely to achieve their ambitions. Poor school performance associated with low-quality schooling, violence exposure and inability to attend school regularly due to work and other responsibilities dampens aspirations and reduces the incentive to remain at school. Adolescence is when gender-based differences emerge most strongly. Concerns over the shortage of work for young people after longer years of school, combined with pressures associated with family poverty, is one of the most important reasons for early school departure, especially among boys. On the other hand, girls have fewer labour market opportunities and are more likely to leave school to form new families. But given the complexity of gendered experiences in adolescence, it is important that policies avoid simplistic assumptions and to recognise that gender analysis requires attention to both girls and to boys.

Key steps include viewing adolescence as a second window for policy in which disadvantages accumulated in early and middle childhood can be addressed, and resilience can be fostered. Interventions related to nutrition may promote growth recovery, with positive effects on wider development. It is also particularly important to support young people as they balance work and education. Flexible schooling schedules may better accommodate working adolescents who face increasing responsibility within their households. Interventions such as cash transfers may reduce the economic necessity of adolescent work. Attention must be paid to school quality, which has implications for school retention, adolescent wellbeing and future employment. Responses to children's work need to be locally relevant and flexible. Without solid evidence of harm, work should not be criminalised or stigmatised. It is also important to ensure that young people have access to safe learning environments. This includes a series of practical steps, such as providing functional gender-segregated toilets, safe transportation for young women, and interventions to reduce corporal punishment and bullying. Retaining girls in school for longer is likely to improve levels of education, but also to reduce early marriage and early childbearing. However, measures to achieve this need to engage with local economic pressures and norms. Many countries face challenges in helping young people enter labour markets. High-quality active labour market policies can help this. Training is likely to have positive gains, though in relation to entrepreneurship these may be greatest when training is linked with other support, such as grants.

Early adulthood sees evidence of the consequences of the earlier developmental cascades. The poorest young people leave school earlier and enter the labour market sooner, resulting in worse labour market conditions and options. The poorest young women are the most likely to marry, cohabit and have children while very young, which reduces the chances of acquiring better education, or good positions in the labour market. Early adulthood is the time when inequalities of outcome of one generation begin to be passed on as inequalities of opportunity to the next. This book has sought to analyse how these disadvantages build up across the first two decades of life, and by doing so to signal key intervention times to improve later chances.

Note

[1] Overweight and obesity are defined using WHO references to body mass index, with obesity a more pronounced form of overweight.

SEVEN

Modelling the development of language and mathematics abilities from early childhood to adolescence

So far the findings outlined in Chapters Four to Six have identified what mattered to Young Lives children during early childhood, middle childhood, adolescence and youth. This chapter examines what mattered *most* during these phases of development. This is done by introducing a new approach, Latent Growth Modelling (LGM), which allows the analysis to go further by simultaneously evaluating multiple paths that affected children's development, over the five survey rounds, and deciding which were relatively more important. The model is applied to the Younger Cohort and the aim is to illustrate the operation of developmental cascades for changes in receptive vocabulary and mathematics abilities. The rationale and a full discussion of technical choices for this LGM analysis has been published separately (Tredoux and Dawes, 2018). These models are especially suitable in the case of Young Lives because they bring together 15 years of longitudinal evidence and are tested across the four study countries. In this chapter, we present the common story, building up from separate country-level analyses. The conclusion to this chapter uses the findings both from the earlier chapters and the modelling presented here to lay out a positive developmental cascade for transitions to adulthood. This provides a framework for action based on Young Lives data, regarding what mattered most and when.

Latent Growth Modelling

The benefit of LGM for present purposes is that we can use the advantage of having five rounds of survey data to examine the longitudinal paths that influenced the development of mathematics abilities and receptive vocabulary. LGMs will not be familiar to all readers and so the approach is set out here. In this case LGM provides a powerful tool for analysing the growth of skills across childhood and adolescence. LGMs extend path model methods to longitudinal research. They use Structural Equation Modelling (SEM) techniques, and have a similar purpose. According to Duncan and Duncan (2009, p 989):

> [LGMs] provide a means of examining (a) whether rates of change differ as a function of growth period (eg early childhood), (b) whether individual variability in rates of change differ between periods (eg from middle childhood to adolescence), and (c) important predictors of change unique to a particular developmental period.

Plausible theoretical models of influences on growth of receptive vocabulary and mathematics abilities during and between each developmental period were constructed, mapped to data and then tested empirically. Not all plausible influences could be tested, as discussed in Tredoux and Dawes (2018). We drew on existing literature, including from Young Lives, to construct the two theoretical models. This made it possible to establish whether these models held up empirically, and which factors influenced the rate of development in mathematics abilities and receptive vocabulary during early and middle childhood and adolescence. There is debate about using causal language in models of this nature. Where the theoretical model is highly plausible (informed by existing evidence), and the empirical test corroborates the model, the case for causal relations in the model is stronger.

The analysis uses data from the Younger Cohort only, and covers the vital early childhood period and middle childhood, with the outcomes gauged at 15 years of age. Future rounds of Young Lives would enable researchers to go further, but it is already known, not least from analysis separately presented in Chapter Six, that these mid-adolescence skills will be crucially important for other later outcomes, not least retention in school, which is then itself related to occurrence of early marriage and quality of parenting.

Growth in receptive vocabulary was measured at 5, 8, 12 and 15 years. In Peru, the norm-referenced Peabody Picture Vocabulary Test (PPVT-R Spanish version; Dunn et al, 1986) was used. In the other countries, where norms did not exist, the tests were based on the PPVT format and administered in the main languages of each country.[1] Reading ability at age 8 years was included to examine the factors in early childhood that influenced this important ability and to assess whether this affected vocabulary growth from 8 years onwards. The effect of the amount of time spent on chores and studying from 8 to 15 years on vocabulary growth, was also included. Finally, at age 15, the influences of vocabulary growth, self-efficacy (Young Lives 'Agency' items), and time spent studying and time spent on chores, on reading comprehension, were tested.

Growth in mathematics ability was assessed through scores on tests administered at 8, 12 and 15 years, with total scores standardised at each round. Standardisation of scores at each round was necessary to construct equivalent scales on the mathematics tests as these differed in the number of items administered at each round. As a result of standardisation, change in children's position on the scale relative to their peers was measured at each round. They could stay in the same position, or improve or regress relative to the others in the sample. We did not use mathematics test items common to all the rounds, as ceiling effects were evident as children aged – particularly for those who were wealthier. The mathematics models explored the influence of quantitative abilities at 5 years of age using the Cognitive Development Assessment (see Cueto et al, 2009). The effect of time for studies and chores and of self-efficacy was also investigated. Full details of all the measures used are presented in Appendix 3, with further information (including reasons for exclusion of certain variables) provided in Tredoux and Dawes (2018).

The two models were tested empirically in each country using data from the household surveys (interviews with the caregivers and the Young Lives study child), and language and mathematics assessments with the children. Blocks of variables were included for early childhood (when children were on average aged 1 year, and when they were 5 years), middle childhood into adolescence (at 8 to 12 years), and in mid- adolescence, when they were 15 years old. Inclusion of variables depended on availability in the questionnaire and suitability of available data for analysis. In early childhood, variables used in all four countries were: material circumstances (the Wealth Index) at 1 and 5 years of age (combined); maternal education and maternal mental health when the child was aged one year; growth stunting at age 1 and 5 years (aggregated); and preschool programme participation in the period 3 to 5 years (programme types varied within and across countries). Information on children's schooling is relevant to the outcomes of interest here. However, since not all children enrolled in the household survey participated in the school surveys, that data could not be included without undermining the power of the analysis through reduced sample sizes. School survey findings from earlier chapters (Chapter Five particularly) should be borne in mind and are drawn in Figure 8.1 in Chapter Eight.

The figures in the following sections illustrate common trajectories across the countries for both receptive vocabulary and mathematics ability. As they cannot be combined across country-level models, coefficients are excluded. Summaries are provided for important cross-country learning and are simplified in a number of ways. Along the top of each figure are the survey rounds and the associated ages of the children. Relationships pictured are not only significant, but of substantive importance. The figures only show significant and important paths (with standardised coefficients greater than 0.15). Solid lines represent relations between variables found in at least three countries. Dotted lines represent relations found in at least two. Arrows show direction, with plus (+) signs indicating positive effects and negative (–) signs indicating negative effects. Thicker lines indicate larger effect sizes, and examples will be given along the way. Hence thick solid lines suggest very important evidence drawn from multiple countries. Variables are marked on the models, those in circles are the latent or growth variables: receptive vocabulary at 5 years old and growth by age 15, and mathematics performance at age 8 and relative change by 15. Blocks between these two represent the components of each latent variable each time this was measured.

Although common findings are presented, the countries differ in the strength of relationships between specific variables for a range of reasons, as discussed in Tredoux and Dawes (2018). The four-country basis of this study provides a way of identifying strong common patterns, to which we now turn.

Determinants of growth in receptive vocabulary

Common findings emerging from the country models of what shapes the growth of receptive vocabulary are set out in Figure 7.1.

In all four countries, wealth status of the household is a strong determinant of outcomes from early childhood onwards. These effects can be seen through a number of channels. Family economic wellbeing in the early years strongly affects children's physical growth at 1 and 5 years of age. This growth in turn affects receptive vocabulary at 5 years old. Stunted children score lower on the test than those with normal growth. The direct effect of poverty (indicated by the solid line) is also evident much later, as it reduces the extent to which children's receptive vocabulary has developed by age 15 (the 'vocab ability slope'), and this influences reading comprehension in adolescence. Importantly, receptive vocabulary at age 5 is also strongly predictive of reading ability in adolescence, showing that success breeds success.

Figure 7.1: Common LGM findings: main influences on the development of receptive vocabulary in Ethiopia, India (UAP), Peru and Vietnam

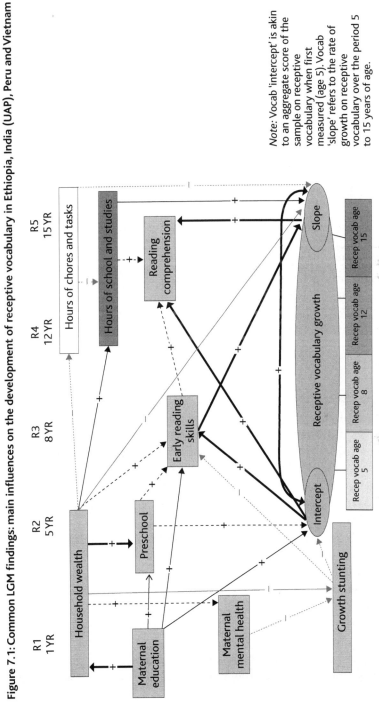

Note: Vocab 'intercept' is akin to an aggregate score of the sample on receptive vocabulary when first measured (age 5). Vocab 'slope' refers to the rate of growth on receptive vocabulary over the period 5 to 15 years of age.

Household wealth also influences preschool access (this variable denotes any early form of learning programme). Preschool access was scaled to take into account probable quality, ranging from no provision, through community-based interventions, to private provision (these sector differences are a proxy since the study does not have learning quality measures). The model shows that better-off children access what are expected to be better early learning programmes (private provision) and that this accrues advantage for early receptive vocabulary and reading at 8 years of age. This does not make an argument for private preschool, but these effects are seen here since this form of service is likely to be better quality in at least two of the countries. In Vietnam, the vast majority of the sample attended state preschools. Children with better-educated mothers are also more likely to attend preschool programmes, and to have enhanced receptive vocabulary and reading skills at age 5 and 8 years respectively. Reading in middle childhood is clearly important as it influences growth in receptive vocabulary to age 15; the two skills mutually reinforce one another. Greater household wealth reduces the amount of time children spend on household chores and increases the time available for school studies.

The relationship between wealth status and outcomes at ages 5 to 12 is generally positive in direction (so greater wealth is associated with better early reading skills, and early receptive vocabulary advantage). However, there is an important exception: the relationship between wealth status and the change in receptive vocabulary between ages 5 and 15 (what is called the 'slope' in the model) is actually negative. This finding means that children from poorer wealth backgrounds showed greater improvement between ages 5 and 15 than was the case for children from wealthier backgrounds. This is due, in part, to the considerably lower performance of children from less wealthy backgrounds at age 5,[2] but it does also show a degree of 'catch-up', probably as a function of exposure to an increased range of vocabulary in school.

The Young Lives study provides an unusual opportunity to explore the relationship between household wealth, maternal psychological wellbeing and child development. Poverty (and associated strain) is known to impact caregiver wellbeing, reducing the emotional energy available for childcare. The LGMs provide evidence of this pattern, showing that when the children were one year-old, women in better off households were less at risk of reporting mental health problems such as anxiety and depression than those who were poorer (dotted line), and children of the latter were also more at risk for growth stunting (dotted line).

The findings confirm that across all the countries early influences are very important. The models also show that the time children spend in school and on after-school studies in middle childhood and adolescence is both influenced by the wealth of their household and has additional consequences for vocabulary development. Unsurprisingly, wealthier children can devote more time to these studying activities and this time is subsequently related to growth in their receptive vocabulary and ultimately to reading comprehension. In contrast, poorer children are more likely to undertake household chores and other responsibilities, and this affects time available for school learning and literacy skills development.

In short, early disadvantage and the reduction of opportunities to learn in middle childhood result in a cascade of negative outcomes for language development through to adolescence. While these findings do suggest the prime importance of the early years, that time to study has additional effects in adolescence and suggests that increasing the opportunities to learn in middle childhood and later would also be likely to have positive consequences for language development.

Determinants of growth in mathematics abilities

This section considers mathematics abilities. The picture for mathematics, set out in Figure 7.2, is simpler than that for receptive vocabulary, but suggests similar influences, including the central importance of the early years. The household-level variables in the mathematics models are the same as for receptive vocabulary. The effects of the household's wealth status on maternal mental health and on growth stunting are evident. As expected, growth status has a negative impact on early quantitative skills. It is plausible that children with better early reading skills are able to understand mathematics problems more readily. This was tested but the variable was intercorrelated with multiple other variables and (so) no clear picture was evident.

The effects of maternal mental health on early quantitative skills and mathematics ability at 8 years old were expected to be mediated by the child's early growth status. This is because, as Young Lives evidence confirms, growth status has a powerful influence on early neurological development and is associated with cognitive growth and mathematics abilities (Grantham-McGregor et al, 2007; Crookston et al, 2013; Duc and Berhman, 2017).

Maternal education levels accrue advantage to children's developing quantitative skills at age 5 years both directly and through the greater

Figure 7.2: Common LGM findings: main influences on the development of mathematics abilities in Peru, India (UAP), Ethiopia and Vietnam

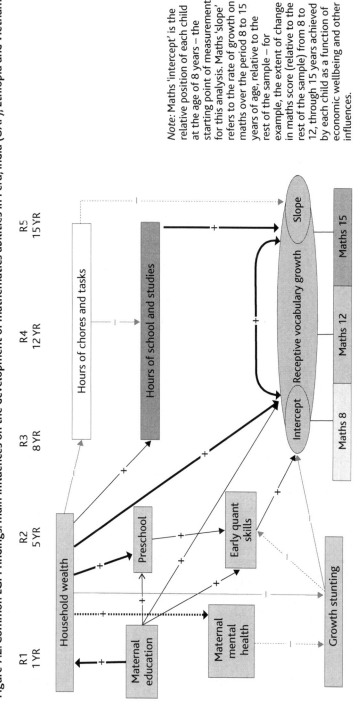

Note: Maths 'intercept' is the relative position of each child at the age of 8 years – the starting point of measurement for this analysis. Maths 'slope' refers to the rate of growth on maths over the period 8 to 15 years of age, relative to the rest of the sample – for example, the extent of change in maths score (relative to the rest of the sample) from 8 to 12, through 15 years achieved by each child as a function of economic wellbeing and other influences.

likelihood that their children will attend a better preschool. That opportunity translates into enhanced cognitive abilities at 5 years old, which in turn enables mathematics abilities at age 8.

Early mathematics skills are strongly predictive of later school success, and those who perform well in early grades continue to stay ahead (Siegler et al, 2012; Watts et al, 2014; Nguyen et al, 2016). While growth in mathematics abilities is influenced by both home and school factors, the role of schooling becomes particularly important as the child ages. This is particularly likely to be the case among children whose parents lack the skills to assist them due to their own limited education – commonly those from poorer households. Such children may be expected to have poorer scores than wealthier children at 8 years, but their skills are likely to grow as they are exposed to school. As noted, it was not possible to include the contribution of schooling in the models. Chapter Five considers the impact of schooling in middle childhood, and suggests national differences in how pro-poor (or otherwise) systems are. Evidence from Vietnam during that age phase suggests the system was able partly to compensate for differences in household background. Evidence from Peru suggests that poorer children get a lower-quality education than richer children in the same schools, implying different patterns of impact for children in different countries.

Children who contribute greater amounts of time to household tasks and chores have less time for their studies. In two countries, more of these responsibilities over the period 8 to 15 years translated into lower growth in mathematics abilities. This shows the continued power of household wealth to influence growth in skills such as mathematics in different ways at early and later periods of development. Opportunities to learn become most important in middle childhood and later.

Common findings: what mattered most for the development of language and mathematics abilities

Modelling the development of language and mathematics in each of the four countries provides unusually powerful cross-country evidence for the importance of a cluster of conditions in early childhood that lay foundations for the development of these skills by mid-adolescence. The paths are broadly similar across the countries, providing cross-national validation of the influences on growth in these cognitive skills. Putting this together, the key factors to emerge are as follows:

- The economic circumstances of the household[3] (measured with the Young Lives Wealth Index) during a child's early years either advantages or places that child at risk for developmental hazards such as illness and growth stunting. Improving the material circumstances of the household (including access to basic services) would therefore be expected to improve a wider set of circumstances, with cumulative effects across the life course.

- Findings from two countries indicate that children whose mothers experience poor mental health because of the stresses of poverty are at risk of poor physical growth in the early years, and that this has a negative impact on language, cognition and numeracy skills. As such, factoring in support to mothers with young children is an important contribution to supporting children themselves.

- Preschool participation was observed to enhance early skill development in terms of receptive vocabulary and quantitative skills, as well as growth in these abilities over time. A range of both public and private preschool programme provision delivered by both professionals and community members was included in the modelling. In some Young Lives countries, private centre-based provision accrued more advantage for literacy skills (early vocabulary and reading) and early quantitative skills and mathematics, than other programme types – not necessarily because they were private, but more that they were likely to be of better quality.

- The models for both mathematics and language indicate that children who perform better on the tests in early childhood continue to do so over time. The models show that these children are from better-off homes and get better early services (preschools) than their less well-off counterparts. Thus, early intervention is likely to be particularly important for poorer children. The implication is that when poor children are provided with the support required for a good start in language and mathematics, they will tend to gain more from later interventions than those who were doing better initially (see also Pfost et al, 2012).

- Finally, disadvantages or advantages are reinforced in middle childhood and adolescence by the extent to which children have to combine household responsibilities with schooling and studying. While findings from Young Lives and other studies confirm the positive contribution of children's activities in support of their families, where these compromise schooling and study time children's academic development is placed at risk. This is most evident for poorer children, whose skill development has in many cases been compromised since the early years. Although that finding points again to the role of early interventions, it also suggests the importance of improving opportunities to learn for poorer children in middle childhood.

Conclusion

From findings presented in previous chapters (and not included in the LGM), we identify social protection and basic services as being relevant to each age phase, but these have a particular role in early childhood.

In terms of what supports children during early childhood, we note the interventions that make a difference, including ensuring that schools are ready for children coming from different backgrounds (such as those needing to work, or speaking a minority first language). During the adolescence phase, we continue to highlight the importance of healthy growth, and add school completion together with being equipped for further education. Again, this suggests the significance of what can improve opportunities to learn, continuing to underscore the value of ensuring safety and gender-appropriate facilities. The importance of the use of institutions (schools and beyond) as platforms to deliver a broader set of activities and services that can support young people is also emphasised.

The implications of this approach for policy are discussed in the Conclusion to the book.

Notes

[1] Analyses of receptive vocabulary on the basis of home language in any country were not separated. In some models, taking home language differences into account would have meant some very small language group samples, which would not have been suitable for this modelling exercise. Moreover, the models reported here do not examine differences between the various home languages in each country. Also, by 15 years, the range of languages in which the children preferred to answer the test had reduced significantly. To maintain consistency over the age points, the majority language of testing at 15 was used. For example, in Peru, it was observed that while the test was taken in both Spanish and indigenous languages at earlier ages, by the age of 15, 95% took the test in Spanish, so that language was chosen for the analyses.

[2] For instance, in United Andhra Pradesh, at age 5, children in the lowest wealth tercile had a mean vocabulary score of 14.9 whereas those in the highest tercile had a mean score of 22.4. At age 15, however, the lowest

wealth tercile had a mean of 45.7 (improving by 30.8 points) while the highest tercile mean was 49.2 (a change of 26.8 points).

3   Household wealth was only included in the models during early childhood as there was little change in relative wealth over the later rounds. This finding does not suggest wealth was unimportant later in childhood. This variable is termed 'economic wellbeing' in the underlying working paper.

EIGHT

Conclusion: Learning from the experiences of Young Lives children

Young Lives has over its five survey rounds, four waves of qualitative research, two school-effectiveness surveys, and several sub-studies, gathered around 150 million items of information on 12,000 children, their caregivers, households, siblings, peers, communities and school classmates. The purpose has been to create a multi-country research resource to be used in understanding the impacts of poverty during childhood in the first two decades of the 21st century. The decision to fund such a study over 15 years was an important contribution to both scientific and policy-relevant knowledge. The future research potential of Young Lives is immense. History shows that cohort studies stimulate insights to questions not even thought of when they began. The study is now a central resource for investigators, policy and practitioner stakeholders, and funders working to extend knowledge of what makes a difference for children's development and wellbeing in low- and middle-income countries (LMICs).

This book has provided an overview of the key findings from a selection of the more than 800 articles and papers published from the study thus far, as well as from original data analysis conducted for this contribution. The volume accompanies country-specific overviews (Cueto et al, 2018; Pankhurst et al, 2018; Singh et al, 2018; Thang and Hang, 2018) and studies on themes of growth and nutrition (Benny et al, 2018), violence affecting children (Pells and Morrow, 2018), child work (Morrow and Boyden, 2018), the labour market (Favara et al, 2018), education (Rossiter et al, 2018) and adolescence (Boyden et al, forthcoming b). The study children grew up in a remarkable period of economic, technological and policy change. Alongside and intimately connected to it, has been social change. A powerful sense of belief in the importance of education to deliver social mobility is present in the words of girls and boys and their parents across the study countries. A more educated and hugely hopeful generation has emerged, one that needs opportunities to realise their aspirations.

A rising tide, but one that didn't lift all boats

The material circumstances experienced by children improved over the course of the study. While progress was sometimes uneven, by the fifth round in 2016 a greater proportion of homes accessed electricity, sanitation and clean water than in 2002. The Young Lives countries also illustrate many social policy successes. Examples include the expansion of basic service access and reductions in chronic under-nutrition, particularly in Peru. Increased access to schooling has been rapid in Ethiopia and in United Andhra Pradesh, where initial access was lower. More girls and greater proportions of the poorest children are now enrolled. Vietnam is notable for its impressive and equitable learning outcomes. Large-scale social protection policies were implemented in all four countries over the course of the study and Young Lives has observed many positive changes for families, children and youth.

But another, more troubling story sits alongside that of overall progress, and it concerns the deep and multifaceted impact of growing up in poverty. The poorest children did least well from the start, and despite economic growth and development, that has not changed over the past two decades,. Poverty sits alongside, and is reinforced by, disadvantage and discrimination on the basis of rural location, gender, minority ethnicity, language, and caste, and low levels of parental education. Poor children often experienced the worst services. In adolescence particularly, poverty and gender interact, and in United Andhra Pradesh adolescent girls are consistently disadvantaged, with those from the poorest households often facing grave deprivations.

Poverty and associated disadvantage creates risks: family ill health, debt, the need for parents to work long hours, or to migrate for work, increases the requirement that children assist their families by fulfilling household responsibilities and working from middle childhood onward. Pressures to work rise appreciably during adolescence, especially for the poorest children. These demands have to be balanced alongside and sometimes at the expense of schooling and educational progress. And while access to education has significantly improved across all the countries, in all except Vietnam more disadvantaged children experience poorer-quality schooling, undermining their potential for skill development, and thwarting earlier aspirations for education to deliver a better life. Although analysis of data from the fifth round is still at the initial stage, it is already clear that poorer children in the Older Cohort left education before their better-off peers, and were concentrated in less well-paid jobs. In this sense, Young Lives evidence confirms the importance of the three priority challenges identified in the Introduction to this book: tackling rising inequality, which bears down progressively on those who are multiply disadvantaged; ensuring that progress in child survival translates into children thriving; and building on strong foundations established in early childhood by sustaining investments through the first two decades of life. The following discussion summarises some ways in which policy can address these challenges.

Untangling the multidimensionality of children's lives

Understanding how poverty in childhood that begins in the early years can have compounding effects at different points in the life cycle, through developmental cascades, can be helpful in demonstrating the possibilities for continuous support to child development. It is a way to analyse and then respond to the complex multidimensionality of children's development, which entails multiple attributes that interact within developmental periods and across time. For example, a caregiver who is burdened by poverty and domestic violence, and is very distressed, may struggle to provide the quality of care she desires to provide for her infant. A consequence could be malnutrition, which affects neurological development, in turn compromising cognitive functioning and skills development at school, as well as undermining emotional wellbeing and a secure sense of self. In adolescence, failing to progress in school together with the rising costs of education may lead to intermittent attendance and early departure, dashing individual and family ambitions for a better future. It is untangling this multidimensionality that helps identify links with 'multiplier effects' over the life course, and therefore points to good opportunities for intervention to mitigate or remediate lost potential.

The clearest message emerging from Young Lives so far is that early investments are essential but not sufficient. There are opportunities to improve outcomes at later points in the life cycle. Across all stages, household poverty is at the root of much of what reduces the realisation of human potential: in the main, improving household economic circumstances means expanding coverage of social protection. The foundation of effective children's policy must in the first place be the promotion of sound early physical and psychological development. Maternal health and wellbeing, child health, food security, improved sanitation, safe drinking water and poverty reduction when children are very young, are all important. Since early healthy growth is predictive of later growth, school readiness and later learning, improving access to effective early services is likely to activate multiplier effects. But other life phases also matter, especially for those who are disadvantaged at the start. In middle childhood, improving children's chances of learning basic skills requires a combination of measures – both at school and at home. Part of that challenge means reforming elements of the education system, such as pedagogic methods and language of instruction, and improving violence prevention, infrastructure, school management and accountability. But it is also about reducing the work burdens that weigh most heavily on poor children through middle childhood and adolescence.

In adolescence, rapid changes in children's brains, bodies and psychological functioning, rising responsiveness to change and the assumption of new roles and responsibilities create opportunities for improved outcomes. Accordingly, this period is now recognised as a second critical window for policy intervention. In that regard, retention in education by mid-adolescence benefits all children, but girls in particular. In United Andhra Pradesh, girls were less likely to be in schools at that point than boys, but actually more likely than boys to be in school in both Ethiopia and Vietnam. In Vietnam, greater enrolment among girls persists through adolescence and into advanced stages of education. In rural Ethiopia, boys may have more economic opportunities during adolescence than girls, although boys are more likely than girls to be in post-school education. At the same time, risks such as violence exposure in and on the way to school constitute barriers to educational advancement and retention as much as to wider health and development (Favara and Sanchez, 2017).

Qualitative interviews with children and parents reveal how opportunities in childhood are shaped by future expectations. Young people talked to Young Lives interviewers about education being important because it leads to better jobs. However, if jobs are not forthcoming, high hopes are unlikely to be sustained; indeed, Young Lives has traced a steady decline in young people's aspirations in many contexts as they pass through their teens. As the returns from education diminish and the demands of work grow, children may lose hope and leave school – boys sometimes earlier than girls. Better education may even have unintended adverse consequences. For example, in United Andhra Pradesh, women have constrained opportunities in the adult labour market and educated daughters may find it harder to obtain a husband. In that context, it should be no surprise if parents do not invest as much in education for their daughters as for their sons.

Differences between poorer children and their better-off peers are very evident in the first decade of life and continue in the second.

They are often compounded by gender distinctions, which tend to emerge in nationally specific ways. Across all the four countries, girls are more likely to partner and have children young. In United Andhra Pradesh, girls experience systematic discrimination across all aspects of life.

Priority investments for children start young

What, then, does this evidence suggest for the priority package of interventions to support improved chances for poor children? Where should limited resources be invested to greatest effect? This is a central question for governments and for advocates for children and it requires national answers that reflect the evidence from research alongside financing and capacity and political feasibility. We can offer some indicators from the research examined here. To identify priorities, we constructed latent growth models (LGM), which cover the period up to middle adolescence. These tested which moments in children's lives and which domains of their development were most important for achievement across the four countries, identifying early and potent factors with cascades of later effects (see Figure 8.1). The analysis points to a number of high-value investments and these are a good place to start: if countries do not have these building blocks in place, other social policies may be undermined.

Figure 8.1 groups Young Lives findings presented throughout this book that are pertinent to each age phase, along with identifying factors that matter throughout (including household poverty, social protection and basic services). It provides a framework to guide action, directing attention to the points in childhood where policy needs to reach to have a high impact in supporting later chances and good transitions to adulthood. Accordingly, there is a second row, which directs attention to what is likely to make the most difference during each phase of children's development.

The framework emphasises the key importance of the early years. As part of what makes a difference, we note the importance of nutrition, early care and high-quality preschool. We also note the importance of family and maternal circumstances, including mental health, education and a reduction in violence.

At the highest level, Young Lives findings show that there are good priority investments but no single 'magic bullet'. Investments across the life course can be best supported by provision of basic services alongside poverty reduction measures. We emphasise five key priorities as follows:

Figure 8.1: Promoting a positive development cascade for child and adolescent development: a framework for action

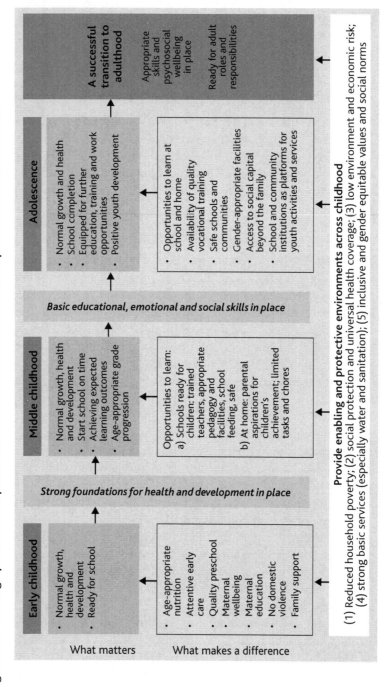

- Expand social protection across childhood and adolescence, starting with families who are the poorest and have the youngest children. Many countries recognise this as a key investment, but coverage often remains low. There is a growing literature on 'child-sensitive' and 'cash-plus' approaches to social protection. This literature contributes lessons on the design of interventions to maximise benefits. Progressive realisation of greater coverage of social protection measures (including universal health coverage) provides a foundation for the success of sector-specific measures, including health, education and child protection.

- Start strong in early childhood. Good early circumstances have long-term consequences. Greater priority should be given to early environments that are nurturing and safe. Supporting children means supporting mothers through interventions that can relieve the stresses they face. It is important to capitalise on the growing wave of interest in preschool as a means of increasing the effectiveness of basic education investments and skills development.

- Support opportunities to learn basic skills in middle childhood. The school is central to modern childhood and provides both an opportunity for learning and a platform for delivery of other programmes. But often, poor children have limited opportunities to learn basic skills. Teaching quality is frequently inadequate, infrastructure of schools poor and environments unsafe or not conducive to learning. Poorer children also face great pressures beyond the school gates. Improving opportunities to learn, including investment in good-quality teaching and safer, more respectful school environments, is central to the development of universal basic skills and human potential. Vietnam's comparative success shows that it can be done.

- Capitalise on adolescence as a second policy window. There is rising recognition of the potential of this period for supporting and enhancing health and development. But the concerns of this group go beyond those often prioritised in policy, for example sexual and reproductive health, and must include healthy growth and positive pro-social relationships, alongside quality schooling and meaningful opportunities for future economic wellbeing. The largest generation of young people ever is also perhaps the most optimistic, but for their aspirations to be realised, the challenge is to deliver quality and relevant services, decent work and entrepreneurial openings. There are hugely positive prospects both for the individual young people and for their societies if this can be realised.

- Meet hopes for social mobility through the new and better opportunities that young people are demanding. Expectations that greater access to schooling will result in greater social mobility are widespread but often not realised. Gender inequalities that are firmly entrenched in the labour market will shape earlier choices over who stays in school and for how long. Job creation is likely to require targeted investments (such as in key infrastructure) and active labour market policies, including vocational training, that increase access to decent jobs and eradicate the worst forms of work. Entrepreneurial schemes may work best when they combine efforts to increase knowledge with grants. Creating access to decent jobs and livelihoods is a huge challenge in many countries, but the availability of such opportunities is key to fulfilling hopes.

Effective systems need capacity, coverage and funds

Policy and programme delivery faces challenging realities in countries where both financing and capacity are often seriously constrained. These challenges have the potential to impede realisation of Sustainable Development Goal (SDG) targets regarding the young. Good systems need effective capacity, sound coverage and sufficient funds. Overloading systems with new demands without capacity improvements may undermine existing essential programmes. The logical response to the multidimensionality of children's development has often been to call for integration, frequently referencing models employed in early childhood. But integration can mean different things depending on context and feasibility. It may involve aligning different sectors to support each other or local coordination and collaboration in services, such as using the school as a platform for the delivery of growth monitoring or feeding. While budget constraints are clearly real, countries still have choices to make, which include: to what extent do they invest in children; what aspects of children's wellbeing do they invest in; and what is to inform these choices? Where budget allocations are made, how pro-poor and how pro-child and gender-equitable are they? Choices must be informed by evidence for what is likely to make the greatest difference to preventing and ameliorating risks, and maximising opportunities for the majority of children's wellbeing and development. The priority areas noted are intended to help inform such debates.

Many governments will continue to face severe constraints on resources and capacity over the SDG period. As economies, the numbers of children, adolescents and youth and awareness of their

152

needs grow, it is essential to make greater space for investments in their development. Effective investments not only secure children and young people's rights, but grow human capital, contributing to the future of whole societies. We identify three approaches toward the progressive realisation of better policies for the young:

- Where choices are to be made between age groups, the most equitable solutions will prioritise young children. This is not to say that older phases of childhood and adolescence are not important, but from an equity and efficiency point of view, if investments in the early years and in school are not sufficient, few will reach their potential.
- Addressing the holistic nature of children's development and the many factors that shape it requires better coordination across sectors such as health, education and social protection. There are challenges to integrated delivery and these need to be addressed pragmatically. Where capacity is limited, calls for service integration may be a step too far. It is better to focus on achievable steps in this direction, ranging from national plans, supported by finance ministries, to encourage synergies between service areas (for example, the expansion of health services or school feeding in primary schools), and cooperation and co-location at a local level between schools, health facilities or other appropriate community infrastructure.
- Effective monitoring is a strategy to support better quality services. 'Quality' within public services is a touchstone for many governments and donors. Quality requires resources (financial and people) and can also be supported by monitoring systems that direct attention to how public services benefit (or not) the poorest children. Identifying and building on existing good practice within countries provides a road map to help achieve quality.

A postscript on the experience of running a comparative cohort study

Behind the Young Lives findings lies the story of the study itself. This book would not be complete without a brief review of what has been learned through carrying out the study, this being particularly important, since Young Lives is rare as both a long-term and comparative study.[1] We end this book on six key reflections from the Young Lives study.

First is the value of **talking to children themselves in both qualitative and survey research**. While this is more common in qualitative research, there are remarkably few surveys that interview children directly. UNICEF's Multiple Indicator Cluster survey[2] approach relies on interviews with caregivers; the widely used Demographic and Health Survey[3] typically only surveys those aged 15 and older. Young Lives and the Children's Worlds surveys[4] are notable exceptions. Not only is it possible to produce useful results by interviewing children in large surveys, but their involvement is necessary for understanding the detail of their lives, such as why children miss out on schooling, what they see as risks, and the protective factors in their lives. While qualitative techniques are important for this kind of information, without surveys it would not be possible to draw statistical links between children's circumstances and their hopes and fears for the future.

Second is the value of **multidisciplinary perspectives for public policy research**. Child development and child poverty are complex and multi-layered concerns, and researching these topics requires the skills and perspectives of diverse approaches and disciplines from across the developmental, medical and social sciences. The Young Lives team reflects multiple disciplinary skills and perspectives, this collaboration having supported a deeper understanding of what matters for children and enabled the use of mixed qualitative and quantitative methods, thereby strengthening the rigour and scope of analysis and reaching wider audiences.

Third is the centrality of maintaining **respectful and effective engagement with research participants**, which is a vital ethical principle and also helps reduce attrition. The quality of the Young Lives data and integrity of the sample has relied on the willingness of children and households to continue as part of the study over its duration. National teams have taken responsibility for cohort maintenance, which requires intensive efforts to keep in touch with participants between rounds, following participants who have moved, and maintaining respectful and trusting relationships with children and their families, including through the sharing of key findings from the research. This, in turn, has required sustained investment in fieldwork capacity through training and, whenever possible, retaining the same field supervisors and fieldworkers over many rounds. The expansion of new technologies (especially mobile phones) allows new avenues of communication, but does not replace the need for sustained fieldwork investment.

Fourth is the importance of **long-term partnerships for effective research and policy engagement**. For research to have policy impact, it needs solid evidence delivered through diverse high-quality outputs, from publications to social media. It also requires that researchers and their evidence become a trusted source for policy audiences. The longevity of engagement and partnership between researchers, advocates, policy-makers and programme staff, especially at national level, has enhanced opportunities for the study to influence thinking and practice. In the case of Young Lives, these long-term partnerships were made possible because of the stability in staffing and institutional arrangements achieved through core funding provided by the UK's Department for International Development and also the value added by support from other donors.

Fifth is the usefulness of **international comparison and the balance between this and national specificity**. The multi-country design has made Young Lives complex to administer, but reveals important similarities and differences in trends across the countries, making it possible to discern the extent to which findings are likely to hold elsewhere. This comparative approach relies on harmonisation of research instruments whenever possible. Undoubtedly there is a tension between this comparative approach and one that uses research instruments tailored to local contexts, such as the use of cognitive tests that are linked to national curricula and address specific national concerns. Young Lives has sought to strike a balance by situating the national experience within a comparative framework, also including country-specific modules in its questionnaires and enquiring about country concerns in the longitudinal qualitative research and sub-studies.

Finally, it is important to value **the type of knowledge a study like Young Lives generates**. Young Lives is a multipurpose observational study that was set up with the aim of informing policy and programming. Although driven by a broad hypothesis about the relation between poverty and children's development and wellbeing, the study was not designed to answer specific questions. There are many advantages to this kind of open-ended inquiry, since it can provide vital new knowledge in areas not anticipated at the start. An important example is the discovery of post-infancy recovery and faltering in physical growth and its association with cognitive gains. If growth recovery can be supported, this would improve the lives of many millions of children. But there are limitations; this finding generates further information needs regarding the most effective remedial investments and multi-purpose observational studies are unable to address these additional questions. Thus, while multi-purpose longitudinal observational research provides vital information to support policy prioritisation, it is most effective when followed up by, or integrated with, intervention studies aimed at informing policy and programme design and maximising intervention impact. Ultimately, the greater impact of Young Lives may well be beyond the achievement of instrumental change and more in challenging assumptions and shifting conceptual knowledge – for example, in emphasising the importance of structural drivers, such as poverty, rurality and social discrimination, over individual attributes in school performance and outcomes. Young Lives is a resource that can be used by future researchers to extend the boundaries of what is known about children, poverty and human development. For social science, it remains crucial that there is scope and funding for this kind of long-term investigative and observational research (ESRC, 2018).

Notes

[1]   Young Lives has been a leader in exploring approaches to research ethics involving children in LMICs (for example, Morrow, 2013b). Research instruments and methodological choices are set out in technical notes, which together with the Young Lives theory of change (Young Lives, 2015b) and information on the impact of the research are available on the Young Lives website: www.younglives.org.uk

[2]   http://mics.unicef.org

[3]   www.dhsprogram.com

[4]   www.isciweb.org

References

Aber, J.L., Gephart, M.A., Brooks-Gunn, J. and Connell, J.P. (1997) 'Development in context: Implications for studying neighborhood effects', in J. Brooks-Gunn, G.J. Duncan and J.L. Aber (eds) *Neighborhood policy. Volume 1: Context and consequences for children* (pp 44-61), New York: Russell Sage Foundation.

Alderman, H. and Walker, S. (2014) 'Enhancing resilience to nutritional shocks', 2020 Conference Brief 17, 17-19 May, Addis Ababa, Ethiopia and Washington, DC: International Food Policy Research Institute (IFPRI) (http://ebrary.ifpri.org/cdm/ref/collection/p15738coll2/id/128139).

Ames, P. and Rojas, V. (2010) *Change and opportunity: The transition from primary to secondary school in rural and urban Peru*, Working Paper 63, Oxford: Young Lives.

Araya, R., Rojas, G., Fritsch, R., Gaete, J., Rojas, M., Simon, G. and Peters, T.J. (2003) 'Treating depression in primary care in low-income women in Santiago, Chile: A randomised controlled trial', *The Lancet*, 361(9362), 995-1000.

Atkinson, A. (2016) *Inequality: What can be done?*, Cambridge, MA: Harvard University Press.

Aurino, E. and Burchi, F. (2014) *Children's multidimensional health and medium-run cognitive skills in low- and middle-income countries*, Working Paper 129, Oxford: Young Lives.

Aurino, E. and Morrow, V. (2018) '"Food prices were high, and the dal became watery". Mixed-method evidence on household food insecurity and children's diets in India', *World Development*, 111, 211-24.

Aurino, E., James, Z. and Rolleston, C. (2014) *Young Lives Ethiopia school survey 2012-13, Data overview report*, Working Paper 134, Oxford: Young Lives.

Aurino, E., Schott, W., Penny, M.E. and Behrman, J.R. (2017) 'Birth weight and prepubertal body size predict menarcheal age in India, Peru, and Vietnam', *New York Academy of Sciences*, 1416(1), 107-16.

Bailey, D., Duncan, G.J., Odgers, C.L. and Yu, W. (2017) 'Persistence and fadeout in the impacts of child and adolescent interventions', *Journal of Research on Educational Effectiveness*, 10(1), 7-39.

Baird, S., Ferreira, F.H.G., Özler, B. and Woolcock, M. (2013) 'Relative effectiveness of conditional and unconditional cash transfers for schooling outcomes in developing countries: A systematic review', *Campbell Systematic Reviews*, 2013(8), 1-124.

Bennett, I.M., Schott, W., Krutikova, S. and Behrman, J.R. (2016) 'Maternal mental health, and child growth and development, in four low-income and middle-income countries', *Journal of Epidemiology and Community Health*, 70(2), 168-73.

Benny, L., Dornan, P. and Georgiadis, A. (2017) *Maternal undernutrition and childbearing in adolescence and offspring growth and development: Is adolescence a critical window for interventions against stunting?*, Working Paper 165, Oxford: Young Lives.

Benny, L., Penny, M. and Boyden, J. (2018) *Early is best but it's not always too late: Young Lives evidence on nutrition and growth in Ethiopia, India, Peru and Vietnam*, Oxford: Young Lives.

Biersteker, L., Dawes, A., Hendricks, L. and Tredoux, C. (2016) 'Center-based early childhood care and education program quality: A South African study', *Early Childhood Research Quarterly*, 36, 334-44.

Bourdillon, M., Levinson, D., Myers, W. and White, B. (2011) *The rights and wrongs of child work*, New Brunswick, NJ: Rutgers University Press.

Boyden, J. (2012) 'Why are current efforts to eliminate female circumcision in Ethiopia misplaced?', *Culture, Health and Sexuality*, 14(10), 1111-23.

Boyden, J. (2013) '"We're not going to suffer like this in the mud": Educational aspirations, social mobility and independent child migration among populations living in poverty', *Compare: A Journal of Comparative and International Education*, 43(5): 580-600.

Boyden, J. and Howard, N. (2013) 'Why does child trafficking policy need to be reformed? The moral economy of children's movement in Benin and Ethiopia', *Children's Geographies*, 11(3), 354-368.

Boyden, J., Pankhurst, A. and Tafere, Y. (2012) 'Child protection and harmful traditional practices: Female early marriage and genital modification in Ethiopia', *Development in Practice*, 22(4), 510-22.

Boyden, J., Porter, C., Zharkevich, I. and Heissler, K. (2016) *Balancing school and work with new opportunities: Changes in children's gendered time use in Ethiopia (2006-2013)*, Working Paper 161, Oxford: Young Lives.

Boyden, J., Espinoza-Revollo, P., Morrow, V. and Porter C. (forthcoming a) *Evolving time use of boys and girls growing up in Ethiopia, India, Peru and Vietnam, 2006-2016*, Oxford, September 2018.

Boyden, J., Ford, K., Walnicki, D. and Winter, F. (forthcoming b) *Investment in adolescents is central to gender equality and eradicating poverty: Young Lives and the realities of adolescence in the 21st century*, Oxford: Young Lives Summative Report.

Brechwald, W.A. and Prinstein, M.J. (2011) 'Beyond homophily: A decade of advances in understanding peer influence processes', *Journal of Research on Adolescence*, 21(1), 166-79.

Brims, F. and Chauhan, A. (2005) 'Air quality, tobacco smoke, urban crowding and day care: Modern menaces and their effects on health', *Pediatric Infectious Disease Journal*, 24(11), s152-s158.

Briones, K. (2017) *How many rooms are there in your house? Constructing the Young Lives Wealth Index*, Technical Note 43, Oxford: Young Lives.

Britto, P.R., Yoshikawa, H. and Boller, K. (2011) 'Quality of early childhood development programs in global contexts: Rationale for investment, conceptual framework and implications for equity', *Social Policy Report*, 25(2) 1-31.

Brody, C., De Hoop, T., Vojtkova, M., Warnock, R., Dunbar, M., Murthy, P. and Dworkin, S.L. (2016) *Economic self-help group programmes for improving women's empowerment: A systematic review*, 3ie Systematic Review 23, London: International Initiative for Impact Evaluation (3ie).

Bronfenbrenner, U. and Morris, P. (2006) 'The bioecoloigical model of human development', in R.M. Lerner and W. Damon (eds) *Handbook of child psychology. Volume 1: Theoretical models of human development* (5th edn, pp 793-828), New York: Wiley.

Bundy, D., de Silva, N., Horton, S., Patton, G., Schultz, L. and Jamison, D. (2018) 'Investment in child and adolescent health and development: Key messages from *Disease Control Priorities*, 3rd Edition', *The Lancet*, 391, 687-99.

Cameron, L. (2009) *Does 'improved' sanitation make children healthier? Household pit latrines and child health in rural Ethiopia*, Working Paper 42, Oxford: Young Lives.

Cho, Y. and Honorati, M. (2014) 'Entrepreneurship programs in developing countries: A meta regression analysis', *Labour Economics*, 28, 110-30.

Chuta, N. (2014) *Childen's agency in responding to shocks and adverse events in Ethiopia*, Working Paper 128, Oxford: Young Lives.

Clark, C., Martin, R., van Kempen, E., Alfred, T., Head, J., Davies, H.W., et al (2006) 'Exposure-effect relations between aircraft and road traffic noise exposure at school and reading comprehension: The RANCH project', *American Journal of Epidemiology*, 163, 27-37.

Concha, J. (2017) *Assessment of the significant contextual changes in the Young Lives countries between 2000 and 2017*, Unpublished Young Lives Background Paper.

Cooper, P.J., Landman, M., Tomlinson, M., Molteno, C., Swartz, L. and Murray, L. (2002) 'Impact of a mother–infant intervention in an indigent peri-urban South African context: Pilot study', *British Journal of Psychiatry*, 180(1), 76–81.

Crivello, G. (2011) '"Becoming somebody": Youth transitions through education and migration in Peru', *Journal of Youth Studies*, 14(4), 395-411.

Crivello, G. and Boyden, J. (2011) *Situating risk in young people's social and moral relationships: Young Lives research in Peru*, Young Lines Working Paper No 66, Oxford May.

Crivello, G. and Morrow, V. (forthcoming) *Against the odds: Why some children fare well in the face of adversity*, Oxford: Young Lives.

Crivello, G. and van der Gaag, N. (2016) *Between hope and a hard place: Boys and young men negotiating gender, poverty and social worth in Ethiopia*, Working Paper 159, Oxford: Young Lives.

Crivello, G. and Espinoza-Revollo, P. (2018) 'Care labour and temporal vulnerability in woman–child relations', in R. Rosen and K. Twamley (eds) *Feminism and the politics of childhood: Friends or foes?*, London: UCL Press.

Crivello, G., Roest, J., Vennam, U. and Singh, R. (2018) *Marital and fertility decision-making: The lived experiences of adolescents and young married couples in Andhra Pradesh and Telangana, India*, Oxford: Young Lives Report.

Crookston, B.T., Penny, M.E., Alder, S.C., Dickerson, T.T., Merrill, R.M., Stanford, J.B., et al (2010) 'Children who recover from early stunting and children who are not stunted demonstrate similar levels of cognition', *The Journal of Nutrition*, 140(11), 1996-2001, https://doi.org/10.3945/jn.109.118927.

Crookston, B.T., Schott, W., Cueto, S., Dearden, K.A., Engle, P., Georgiadis, A., et al (2013) 'Post-infancy growth, schooling, and cognitive achievement: Young Lives', *The American Journal of Clinical Nutrition*, 98(6), 1555-63.

Cueto, S. and Leon, J. (2012) *Psychometric characteristics of cognitive development and achievement instruments in round 3 of Young Lives*, Technical Note 25, Oxford: Young Lives.

Cueto, S., Escobal, J., Felipe, C., Pazos, N., Penny, M., Rojas, V. and Sánchez, A. (2018) *¿Qué hemos aprendido del estudio longitudinal Niños del Milenio en el Perú? Síntesis de hallazgos* [*What have we learned from the longitudinal study Young Lives in Peru? Summary of findings*], Lima: Niños del Milenio.

Cueto S., Escobal J., Penny, M. and Ames, P. (2011) *Tracking disparities: Who gets left behind? Initial findings from PERU round 3 survey report*, Oxford: Young Lives.

Cueto, S., Guerrero, G., Leon, J., Zapata, M. and Freire, S. (2014) 'The relationship between socioeconomic status at age one, opportunities to learn and achievement in mathematics in fourth grade in Peru', *Oxford Review of Education*, 40(1), 50-72.

Cueto, S., Leon, J., Guerrero, G. and Muñoz, I. (2009) *Psychometric characteristics of cognitive development and achievement instruments in round 2 of Young Lives*, Technical Note 15, Oxford: Young Lives.

Cueto, S., Leon, J., Miranda, A., Dearden, K., Crookston, B. and Behrman, J. (2015) 'Does pre-school improve cognitive abilities among children with early-life stunting? A longitudinal study for Peru', *International Journal of Educational Research*, 75(2016), 102-14.

Cueto, S., Singh, S., Woldehanna, T., Duc, L. and Miranda, A. (2016) *Education trajectories in Ethiopia, India, Peru and Vietnam: From early childhood to early adulthood*, Policy Brief 30, Oxford: Young Lives.

Dahl, G. and Lochner, L. (2005) *The impact of family income on child achievement*, NBER Working Paper 11279, Cambridge, MA: National Bureau of Economic Research.

Dang, H. and Glewwe, P. (2017) *Well begun, but aiming higher: A review of Vietnam's education trends in the past 20 years and emerging challenges*, Policy Research Working Paper 8112, Washington, DC: The World Bank.

Davis, O.S.P., Band, G., Pirinen, M., Haworth, C.M.A., Meaburn, E.L., Kovas, Y., et al (2014) 'The correlation between reading and mathematics ability at age twelve has a substantial genetic component', *Nature Communications*, 5, https://doi.org/10.1038/ncomms5204.

De Onis, M. and Branca, F. (2016) 'Childhood stunting: A global perspective', *Maternal & Child Nutrition*, 12(Suppl 1), 12-26.

Dercon, S. and Sánchez, A. (2013) 'Height in mid childhood and psychosocial competencies in late childhood: Evidence from four developing countries', *Economics and Human Biology*, 11(4), 426-43.

Dercon, S. and Singh, A. (2013) 'From nutrition to aspirations and self-efficacy: Gender bias over time among children in four countries', *World Development*, 45, 31-50.

Diaz, J. (2006) *Pre-school education and schooling outcomes in Peru*, Niños del Milenio (www.grade.org.pe/upload/publicaciones/archivo/download/pubs/preschool_jjd.pdf).

Dornan, P. (2010) *Understanding the impacts of crisis on children in developing countries*, Young Lives Round 3 Preliminary Findings, Oxford: Young Lives.

Dornan, P. and Boyden, J. (2011) *Putting children at the centre of poverty debate*, Policy Brief No 12, Oxford: Young Lives.

Dornan, P. and Georgiadis, A, (2015) *Nutrition, stunting and catch-up growth*, Policy Brief no. 27, Oxford: Young Lives.

Dornan, P. and Woodhead, M. (2015) *How inequalities develop through childhood: Life course evidence from the Young Lives cohort study*, Office of Research Discussion Paper 2015-01, Florence: UNICEF Office of Research.

Duc, L.T. and Tam T.M.N. (2015) *Growth in middle childhood and early adolescence, and its association with cognitive and non-cognitive skills at the age of 15 years: Evidence from Vietnam*, Working Paper 138, Oxford: Young Lives.

Duncan, T.E. and Duncan, S.C. (2009) 'The ABCs of LGM: An introductory guide to latent variable growth curve modeling', *Social and Personality Psychology Compass*, 3(6), 979-91.

Duncan, G.J., Dowsett, C.J., Claessens, A., Magnuson, K., Huston, A.C., Klebanov, P., et al (2007) 'School readiness and later achievement', *Developmental Psychology*, 43(6), 1428.

Duncan, G.J., Ziol-Guest, K.M. and Kalil, A. (2010) 'Early-childhood poverty and adult attainment, behavior and health', *Child Development*, 81(1), 306-25.

Dunn, L., Padilla, E., Lugo, D. and Dunn, L. (1986) *Manual del examinador para el Test de Vocabulario en Imágenes Peabody: Adaptación Hispanoamericana* [*Peabody Picture Vocabulary Test: Hispanic-American adaptation*], Circle Pines, MN: American Guidance Service.

Duvendack, M., Palmer-Jones, R., Copestake, J.G., Hooper, L., Loke, Y. and Rao, N. (2011) *What is the evidence of the impact of microfinance on the well-being of poor people?*, London: EPPI-Centre, Social Science Research Unit, Institute of Education, University of London.

Eckardt, S., Demombynes, G. and Chandrasekharan Behr, D. (2016) *Vietnam: Systematic country diagnostic*, Washington, DC: The World Bank.

Engle, P.L., Fernald, L.C.H., Alderman, H., Behrman, J., Gara, C.O., Yousafzai, A., et al (2011) 'Child Development 2: Strategies for reducing inequalities and improving developmental outcomes for young children in low-income and middle-income countries', *The Lancet*, 378 (9799), 1339-53.

ESRC (Economic and social Research Council) (2018) *Outline response to 2017 Longitudinal Studies Strategic Review*, Swindon: ESRC.

Escobal, J., Ames, P., Cueto, S., Penny, M. and Flores, E. (2008) *Young Lives: Peru round 2 survey*, Country Report, Oxford: Young Lives.

Escobal, J. and Flores, E (2008) *An assessment of the Young Lives sampling approach in Peru*, Technical Note 3, Oxford: Young Lives.

Espinoza-Revollo, P. and Porter, C. (2018) *Evolving time use of children growing up in Ethiopia, India, Peru and Vietnam, 2006-2016*, Working Paper 180, Oxford: Young Lives.

Evans, D. and Popova, A. (2015) *What really works to improve learning in developing countries? An analysis of divergent findings in systematic reviews*, Policy Research Working Paper 7203, Washington, DC: The World Bank.

Farran, D.C. and Lipsey, M.W. (2015) 'Expectations of sustained effects from scaled up pre-K: Challenges from the Tennessee study', *Evidence Speaks Reports*, 1(3).

Favara, M. (2016) *Do dreams come true? Aspirations and educational attainments of Ethiopian boys and girls*, Working Paper 146, Oxford: Young Lives.

Favara, M. and Sánchez, A. (2017) 'Psychosocial competencies and risky behaviours in Peru', *IZA Journal of Labor & Development*, 6(3), 1-40.

Favara, M., Chang, G. and Sánchez, A. (2018) *No longer children: What do Young Lives children do when they grow up?*, Summative Report, Oxford: Young Lives.

Favara, M., Woodhead, M., Castro, J., Chang, G. and Espinoza-Revollo, P. (forthcoming) *Pre-school education and skills development in Peru, Vietnam, Ethiopia and India: Evidence from Young Lives*, Washington, DC: The World Bank.

Feikin, D.R., Flannery, B., Hamel, M.J., Stack, M. and Hansen, P.M. (2016) 'Vaccines for children in low- and middle-income countries', in R.E. Black, R. Laxminarayan, M. Temmerman and N. Walker (eds) *Reproductive, maternal, newborn, and child health: Disease Control Priorities, Third Edition (Volume 2)* (pp 187-204), Washington, DC: International Bank for Reconstruction and Development/The World Bank.

Fink, G. and Rockers, P.C. (2014) 'Childhood growth, schooling, and cognitive development: Further evidence from the Young Lives study', *American Journal of Clinical Nutrition*, 100(1), 182-8.

Furstenberg, F.F. and Hughes M.E. (1997) 'The influence of neighborhoods on children's development: A theoretical perspective and a research agenda', in J. Brooks-Gunn, G.J. Duncan and J.L. Aber (eds) *Neighborhood policy. Volume 2: Policy implications in studying neighborhoods* (pp 23-47), New York: Russell Sage Foundation.

Galab, S., Kumar, V., Reddy, P., Singh, R. and Vennam, U. (2011) *The impact of growth on childhood poverty in Andhra Pradesh: Initial findings from India*, Oxford: Young Lives.

Galab, S.P., Reddy, P. and Singh, R. (2014) *Education and learning. Preliminary findings from the 2013 Young Lives survey (round 4): United Andhra Pradesh*, Oxford: Young Lives.

Gavidia, T. Pronczuk de Garbino, J. and Sly, P. (2009) 'Children's environmental health: An under-recognised area in paediatric health care', *BMC Pediatrics*, 9, 10.

Gavonel, M. (2017) *Patterns and drivers of internal migration among youth in Ethiopia, India, Peru and Vietnam*, Working Paper 169, Oxford: Young Lives.

Georgiadis, A. (2016) *The sooner the better but it's never too late: The impact of nutrition at different periods of childhood on cognitive development*, Working Paper 159, Oxford: Young Lives.

Georgiadis, A. and Penny, M. (2017) 'Child undernutrition: Opportunities beyond the first 1000 days', *The Lancet Public Health*, 2(9), 399.

Georgiadis, A., Benny, L., Duc, LT., Galab, S., Reddy, P. and Woldehanna, T. (2017) 'Growth recovery and faltering through early adolescence in low- and middle-income countries: Determinants and implications for cognitive development', *Social Science & Medicine*, 179(2017), 81-90.

Glewwe, P., Chen, Q. and Katare, B. (2015) 'What determines learning among Kinh and ethnic minority students in Vietnam? An analysis of the round 2 Young Lives Data', *Asia & The Pacific Policy Studies*, 2(3), 494-516.

Global Coalition to End Child Poverty (2017) *Child-sensitive Social Protection*, Briefing Paper, Global Coalition to End Child Poverty (www.endchildhoodpoverty.org/publications-feed/2017/11/1/9v6 1mcxy3mw336oilgamomko1p12it).

Gove, A. and Wetterberg, A. (2011) *The Early Grade Reading Assessment: Applications and interventions to improve basic literacy*, Durham, NC: Research Triangle Institute.

Government of India (2017) *India Three Year Action Agenda, 2017-18 to 2019-20*, New Delhi: NITI Aayog.

Grantham-McGregor, S., Cheung, Y., Cueto, S., Glewwe, P., Richter, L. and Strupp, B. (2007) 'Developmental potential in the first 5 years for children in developing countries', *The Lancet*, 369, 60-70.

Grantham-McGregor, S.M., Fernald, L.C., Kagawa, R. and Walker, S. (2014) 'Effects of integrated child development and nutrition interventions on child development and nutritional status', *Annals of the New York Academy of Sciences*, 1308(1), 11-32.

Guerrero, G., Leon, J., Zapata, M., Sugimaru, C. and Cueto, S. (2012) *What works to improve teacher attendance in developing countries? A systematic review*, London: EPPI-Centre, Social Science Research Unit, Institute of Education, University of London.

Handa, S., Daidone, S., Peterman, A., Davis, B., Pereira, A., Palermo, T. and Yablonski, J. on behalf of the Transfer Project (2017) *Myth-busting? Confronting six common perceptions about unconditional cash transfers as a poverty reduction strategy in Africa*, Innocenti Working Paper 2017-11, Florence: UNICEF Office of Research.

Hardgrove, A., Pells, K., Boyden, J. and Dornan, P. (2014) *Youth vulnerabilities in life course transitions*, UNDP Occasional Paper, New York: United Nations Development Programme.

Harpham, T., Huttley, S., De Silva, M. and Abramsky, T. (2005) 'Maternal mental health and child nutritional status in four developing countries', *Journal of Epidemiology & Community Health*, 59(12), 1060-4.

Harpham, T., Reichenheim, M., Oser, R. Thomas, E., Hamid, N., Jaswal, S., et al (2003) 'How to do (or not to do): Measuring mental health in a cost-effective manner', *Health and Policy Planning*, 18(3), 344-9.

Haworth, C.M., Wright, M.J., Luciano, M., Martin, N.G., de Geus, E.J., van Beijsterveldt, C.E., et al (2009) 'The heritability of general cognitive ability increases linearly from childhood to young adulthood', *Molecular Psychiatry*, 15(11), 1112-20.

Heissler, K. and Porter, C. (2013) 'Know your place: Ethiopian children's contributions to the household economy', *European Journal of Development Research*, 25(4), 600-20.

Higginson, A., Benier, K., Shenderovich, Y., Bedford, L., Mazerolle, L. and Murray, J. (2015) 'Preventive interventions to reduce youth involvement in gangs and gang crime in low- and middle-income countries: A systematic review', *Campbell Systematic Reviews*, 11(18), 1-176.

Himaz, R. (2018) 'Stunting later in childhood and outcomes as a young adult: Evidence from India', *World Development*, 104, 344-57.

Hoadley, U. (2013) 'Building strong foundations: Improving the quality of early education', in L. Berry, L. Biersteker, H. Dawes, L. Lake and C. Smith C (eds) *South African Child Gauge 2013* (pp 72-7), Cape Town: Children's Institute, University of Cape Town.

Humphries, D.L., Behrman, J.R., Crookston, B.T., Dearden, K.A., Schott, W. and Penny, M.E. (2014) 'Households across all income quintiles, especially the poorest, increased animal source food expenditures substantially during recent Peruvian economic growth', *PLOS One*, 9(11), e110961.

Huong, V. (2011) 'Understanding resilience, risk, and protection in the light of school attendance and dropout: A comparative cross-case analysis on qualitative data in Vietnam', *Vietnam Journal of Family and Gender Studies*, 6(2), 38-50.

ILO (International Labour Organization) (1999) *Convention concerning the Prohibition and Immediate Action for the Elimination of the Worst Forms of Child Labour* (No 182), Adoption: Geneva, 87th ILC session (17 June 1999).

ILO (2017) *World Social Protection Report 2017–19: Universal social protection to achieve the Sustainable Development Goals*, Geneva: ILO.

International Commission on Financing Global Education Opportunity (2018) 'The learning generation: investing in education for a changing world' (http://report.educationcommission.org).

Jensen, R. and Thornton, R. (2003) 'Early female marriage in the developing world', *Gender and Development*, 11(2), 9-19.

Johri, M., Pérez, M., Arsenault, C., Sharma, J., Pai, N., Pahwa, S. and Sylvestrea, M. (2016) 'Strategies to increase the demand for childhood vaccination in low-and middle-income countries: A systematic review and meta-analysis', *Revista Facultad Nacional de Salud Pública*, 34(2), 243-53.

Kabeer, N. (2016) '"Leaving no one behind": The challenge of intersecting inequalities', in ISSC, IDS and UNESCO *World social science report 2016. Challenging inequalities: Pathways to a just world* (Chapter 8, pp 55-8), Paris: UNESCO.

Kalamar, A., Lee-Rife, S. and Hindin, M. (2016) 'Interventions to prevent child marriage among young people in low-and middle-income countries: A systematic review of the published and gray literature', *Journal of Adolescent Health*, 59(3), S16-S21.

Klein, H. (1990) 'Adolescence, youth, and young adulthood', *Youth & Society*, 21(4), 446-71.

Kaufman, J., Synnot, A., Ryan, R., Hill, S., Horey, D., Willis, N., et al (2013) 'Face to face interventions for informing or educating parents about early childhood vaccination', *Cochrane Database of Systematic Reviews*, 5, CD010038, doi:10.1002/14651858.CD010038.pub2.

Kluve, J., Puerto, S., Robalino, D., Romero, J.M., Rother, F., Stöterau, J., et al (2017) *Interventions to improve the labour market outcomes of youth: A systematic review of training, entrepreneurship promotion, employment services and subsidized employment interventions*, 3ie Systematic Review 37, London: International Initiative for Impact Evaluation (3ie).

Knowles, C. and van der Gaag, N. (2009) *'Nothing is impossible for me': Stories from Young Lives children*, Oxford: Young Lives.

Know Violence in Childhood (2017) *Ending violence in childhood. Global report 2017*, New Delhi: Know Violence in Childhood.

Kovas, Y., Haworth, C.M., Dale, P.S. and Plomin, R. (2007) 'The genetic and environmental origins of learning abilities and disabilities in the early school years', *Monographs of the Society for Research in Child Development*, 72(vii), 1-144.

Kristjansson, E., Francis, D., Liberato, S., Greenhalgh, T., Welch, V., Jandu, M.B., et al (2016) *Supplementary feeding for improving the health of disadvantaged infants and young children: A systematic and realist review*, 3ie Systematic Review 15, London: International Initiative for Impact Evaluation (3ie).

Kristjansson, E.A., Robinson, V., Petticrew, M., MacDonald, B., Krasevec, J., Janzen, L., et al (2006) 'School feeding for improving the physical and psychosocial health of disadvantaged students', *Campbell Systematic Reviews*, 14, doi:10.4073/csr.2006.14.

Krutikova, S., Rolleston, C. and Aurino, E. (2014) 'How much difference does school make and for whom? A two-country study of the impact of school quality on educational attainment', in M. Bourdillon and J. Boyden (eds) *Growing up in poverty: Findings from Young Lives* (pp 201-24), Basingstoke: Palgrave Macmillan.

Kumra, N. (2008) *An assessment of the Young Lives sampling approach in Andhra Pradesh, India*, Technical Note 2, Oxford: Young Lives.

Lassi, Z.S., Guleshehwar, Z., Das, J.K. and Bhutta, Z.A. (2013) *Assignment report: Systematic review of complementary feeding strategies amongst children less than two years of age*, Maidenhead: HEART UK.

Le, T.D. and Tran, N.M.T. (2013) *Why children in Vietnam drop out of school and what they do after that*, Oxford: Young Lives.

Lee-Rife, S., Malhotra, A., Warner, A. and McGonagle Glinski, A. (2012) 'What works to prevent child marriage: A review of the evidence', *Studies in Family Planning*, 43(4), 287-303.

Lenhardt, A. and Shepherd, A. (2013) *What has happened to the poorest 50%?*, Working Paper 184, Manchester: Brooks World Poverty Institute.

Lenroot, R.K. and Giedd, J.N. (2011) 'Annual research review: Developmental considerations of gene by environment interactions', *Journal of Child Psychology and Psychiatry*, 52(4), 429-41.

Leon, J. and Singh, A. (2017) *Equating test scores for receptive vocabulary across rounds and cohorts in Ethiopia, India and Vietnam*, Technical Note 40, Oxford: Young Lives.

Lerner, R., Fisher, C. and Weinberg, R. (2000) 'Towards a science for and of the people: Promoting civil society through the application of developmental science', *Child Development*, 71(1), 11-20.

Leroy, J., Ruel, M., Habicht, J. and Frongillo, E. (2015) 'Using height-for-age differences (HAD) instead of height-for-age z-scores (HAZ) for meaningful measurement of population-level catch-up in linear growth in children less than 5 years of age', *BMC Pediatrics*, 15, 145.

Lipina, S.J. and Segretin, M.S. (2015) 'Strengths and weakness of neuroscientific investigations of childhood poverty: Future directions', *Frontiers in Human Neuroscience*, 9, https://doi.org/10.3389/fnhum.2015.00053.

Liu, J. (2011) 'Early health risk factors for violence: Conceptualisation, evidence, and implications', *Aggression and Violent Behavior*, 16, 63-73.

Lund, C., Breen, A., Flisher, A., Kakuma, R., Corrigall, J., Joska, J., et al. (2010) 'Poverty and common mental disorders in low and middle income countries: A systematic review', *Social Science & Medicine*, 71(3), 517-28.

Luthar, S.S., Cicchetti, D. and Becker, B. (2000) 'The construct of resilience: A critical evaluation and guidelines for future work', *Child Development*, 71(3), 543-62.

Male, C. and Wodon, Q. (2016) *Basic profile of early childbirth in Peru*, Health, Nutrition, and Population (HNP) Knowledge Brief: Child Marriage Series, Washington, DC: The World Bank.

Masino, S. and Nino-Zarazua, M. (2015) *What works to improve the quality of student learning in developing countries?*, WIDER Working Paper 2015/033, Tokyo: World Institute for Development Economics Research.

Masten, A. and Cicchetti, D. (2010) 'Developmental cascades', *Development and Psychopathology*, 22, 491-5.

Masten, A.S. (2001) 'Ordinary magic: Resilience processes in development', *American Psychologist*, 56(3), 227-38.

McQueston, K., Silverman, R. and Glassman, A. (2012) *Adolescent fertility in low- and middle-income countries: Effects and solutions*, CGD Working Paper 295, Washington, DC: Center for Global Development.

Morgan, C., Petrosino, A. and Fronius, T. (2012) *A systematic review of the evidence of the impact of eliminating school user fees in low-income developing countries*, London: EPPI-Centre, Social Science Research Unit, Institute of Education, University of London.

Morgan, C., Petrosino, A. and Fronius, T. (2013) *A systematic review of the evidence of the impact of school voucher programmes in developing countries.* London: EOOI-Centre, Social Science Research Unit, Institute of Education, University of London.

Morrow, V. (2013a) 'Troubling transitions? Young people's experiences of growing up in poverty in rural Andhra Pradesh, India', *Journal of Youth Studies*, 16(1), 86-100.

Morrow, V, (2013b) 'Practical ethics in social research with children and families in Young Lives: A longitudinal study of childhood poverty in Ethiopia, Andhra Pradesh (India), Peru and Vietnam', *Methodological Innovations* Online, 8(2), 21-35.

Morrow, V. and Boyden, J. (2018) *Responding to children's work: Evidence from the Young Lives study in Ethiopia, India, Peru and Vietnam*, Summative Report, Oxford: Young Lives.

Morrow, V. and Singh, R. (2014) *Corporal punishment in schools in Andhra Pradesh, India. Children's and parents' views*, Working Paper 123, Oxford: Young Lives

Morrow, V. and Vennam, U. (2015) '"Those who are good to us, we call them friends": Social support and social networks for children growing up in poverty in Rural Andhra Pradesh, India', in L. Alanen, E. Brooker and B. Mayall (eds) *Childhood with Bourdieu* (pp 142-64), Basingstoke: Palgrave Macmilllan.

Morrow, V., Tafere, Y. and Vennam, U. (2014) 'Changes in rural children's use of time: Evidence from Ethiopia and Andhra Pradesh', in M. Bourdillon and J. Boyden (eds) *Growing up in Poverty: Findings from Young Lives* (pp 139-59), Basingstoke: Palgrave Macmillan.

Morrow, V., Tafere, Y., Chuta, N. and Zharkevich, I. (2017) '"I started working because I was hungry": The consequences of food insecurity for children's well-being in rural Ethiopia', *Social Science & Medicine*, 182, 1-9.

Murray, H. and Woodhead, M. (2010) *Early childhood care and education as a strategy for poverty reduction: Evidence from Young Lives*, Policy Brief 9, Oxford: Young Lives.

Myers, R. (2001) 'In search of early childhood indicators', *Coordinators' Notebook*, 25, 3-31.

Myers, R. (2006) *Quality in programmes of early childhood care and education (ECCE). Background paper prepared for the Education for All Global Monitoring Report 2007*, Paris: UNESCO.

Naafs, S. and Skelton, T. (2018) 'Youthful futures? Aspirations, education and employment in Asia', *Children's Geographies*, 16(1), 1–14.

Nagle, B.J., Holub, C.K., Barquera, S., Sanchez-Romero, L.M., Eisenberg, C.M., Rivera-Dommarco, J.A., et al (2013) 'Interventions for the treatment of obesity among children and adolescents in Latin America: A systematic review', *Salud Publica de Mexico*, 55(Suppl 3), 434–40.

Nguyen, N.P. (2008) *An assessment of the Young Lives sampling approach in Vietnam*, Technical Note 4, Oxford: Young Lives.

Nguyen, T., Watts, T.W., Duncan, G.J., Clements, D.H. and Julie, S. (2016) 'Which preschool mathematics competencies are most predictive of fifth grade achievement?', *Early Childhood Research Quarterly*, 36, 550–60.

Nolan, L. (2016) 'Rural–urban child height for age trajectories and their heterogeneous determinants in four developing countries', *Population Research and Policy Review*, 35(5), 599–629.

Nores, M. and Barnett, W. (2010) 'Benefits of early childhood interventions across the world: (Under) investing in the very young', *Economics of Education Review*, 29, 271–82. doi:10.1016/j.econedurev.2009.09.001.

OECD (Organisation for Economic Co-operation and Development) (2016) *PISA 2015. Results (volume I): Excellence and equity in education*, Paris: PISA OECD Publishing.

Ogando Portela, M. and Pells, K. (2015a) 'Risk and protective factors for children experiencing adverse events', in M. Bourdillon and J. Boyden (eds) *Growing up in poverty: Findings from Young Lives* (Chapter 3, pp 71–94), Basingstoke: Palgrave Macmillan.

Ogando Portela, M. and Pells, K. (2015b) *Corporal punishment in schools: Longitudinal evidence from Ethiopia, India, Peru and Vietnam*, Innocenti Discussion Paper 2015-02, Florence: UNICEF Office of Research.

OPHI (Oxford Poverty and Human Development Initiative) (2018) *Global multidimensional poverty index 2019*, Oxford: OPHI.

Orr, D., Westbrook, J., Pryor, J., Durrani, N., Sebba, J. and Adu-Yeboah, C. (2013) *What are the impacts and cost-effectiveness of strategies to improve performance of untrained and under-trained teachers in the classroom in developing countries?*, London: EPPI-Centre, Social Science Research Centre, Institute of Education, University of London.

Outes-Leon, I. and Porter, C. (2013) 'Catching up from early nutritional deficits? Evidence from rural Ethiopia', *Economics and Human Biology*, 11(2), 148–63.

Outes-Leon, I. and Sánchez, A. (2008) *An assessment of the Young Lives sampling approach in Ethiopia*, Technical Note 1, Oxford: Young Lives.

Pankhurst, A. (2014) *Child marriage and female circumcision (FGM/C): Evidence from Ethiopia*, Policy Brief 21, Oxford: Young Lives.

Pankhurst, A. and Tiumelissan, A. (2013) *Living in urban areas due for redevelopment: Views of children and their families in Addis Ababa and Hawassa*, Working Paper 105, Oxford: Young Lives.

Pankhurst, A., Woldehanna, T., Araya, M., Tafere, Y., Rossiter, J., Tiumelissan, A. and Berhanu, K. (2018) *Young Lives Ethiopia: Lessons from longitudinal research with children of the millennium*, Country Report, Oxford: Young Lives.

Parkes J., Heslop, J., Ross, F., Westerveld, R. and Unterhalter, E. (2016) *A rigorous review of global research evidence on policy and practice on school-related gender-based violence*, New York: UNICEF.

Patton, G.C., Sawyer, S.M., Santelli, J.S., Ross, D.A., Afifi, R., Allen, N.B., et al (2016) 'Our future: A Lancet Commission on adolescent health and wellbeing', *The Lancet*, 387(10036), 2423-78.

Pearl, J. (2012) 'The causal foundations of structural equation modeling', in R.H. Hoyle (ed) *Handbook of structural equation modeling* (pp 68-91), New York: Guilford Press,

Pega, F., Liu, S.Y., Walter, S., Pabayo R., Saith, R. and Lhachimi, S.K. (2017) 'Unconditional cash transfers for reducing poverty and vulnerabilities: effect on use of health services and health outcomes in low- and middle-income countries', *Cochrane Database of Systematic Reviews*, 11, CD011135. doi:10.1002/14651858.CD011135.pub2.

Pells, K. (2011a) *Poverty, risk and families' responses: Evidence from Young Lives*, Young Lives Policy Paper 4, Oxford: Young Lives.

Pells, K. (2011b) *Poverty and gender inequalities: Evidence from Young Lives*, Young Lives Policy Paper 3, Oxford: Young Lives.

Pells, K. and Morrow, V. (2018) *Children's experiences of violence: Evidence from the Young Lives study in Ethiopia, India, Peru and Vietnam*, Summative Report, Oxford: Young Lives.

Pells, K. and Woodhead, M, (2014) *Changing children's lives: Risks and opportunities*, Oxford: Young Lives.

Petrosino, A., Morgan, C., Fronius, T., Tanner-Smith, E. and Boruch, R. (2016) *Interventions in developing nations for improving primary and secondary school enrolment of children: A systematic review*, 3ie Systematic Review 3, London: International Initiative for Impact Evaluation (3ie).

Pfost, M., Dörfler, T. and Artelt, C. (2012) 'Reading competence development of poor readers in a German elementary school sample: An empirical examination of the Matthew effect model', *Journal of Research in Reading*, 35(4), 411-26, http://doi.org/10.1111/j.1467-9817.2010.01478.x.

Piketty, T. (2014) *Capital in the twenty-first century*, Cambridge, MA: Harvard University Press.

Pimhidzai, O. (2018) *Climbing the ladder: Poverty reduction and shared prosperity in Vietnam*, Washington, DC: The World Bank.

Pinderhughes, E., Nix, R., Foster, E. and Jones, D. (2001) 'Parenting in context: Impact of neighborhood poverty, residential stability, public services, social networks, and danger on parental behaviors', *Journal of Marriage and Family*, 63(4), 941-53.

Plomin, R. (2018) *Blueprint: How DNA makes us who we are*, Cambridge, MA: MIT Press.

Prendergast, A.J. and Humphrey, J.H. (2014) 'The stunting syndrome in developing countries', *Paediatrics and International Child Health*, 2 November, 34(4), 250-65.

Rahman, A., Malik, A., Sikander, S., Roberts, C. and Creed, F. (2008) 'Cognitive behaviour therapy-based intervention by community health workers for mothers with depression and their infants in rural Pakistan: A cluster-randomised controlled trial', *The Lancet*, 372(9642), 902-9.

Rao, N., Sun, J., Pearson, V., Pearson, E., Liu, H., Constas, M.A. and Engle, P.L. (2012) 'Is something better than nothing? An evaluation of early childhood programs in Cambodia', *Child Development*, 83(3), 864-76.

Richter, L., Victora, C., Hallal, P., Adair, L., Bhargava, S., Fall, C., et al (2012) 'Cohort profile: The Consortium of Health-Orientated Research in Transitioning Societies', *International Journal of Epidemiology*, 41(3), 621-6.

Roelen, K. (2017) 'Monetary and multidimensional child poverty: A contradiction in terms?', *Development and Change*, 48(3), May, 502-33.

Roest, J. (2016) *Child marriage and early child-bearing in India: Risk factors and policy implications*, Young Lives Policy Paper No 10, Oxford: Young Lives.

Rogoff, B. (2003) *The cultural nature of human development*, Oxford: Oxford University Press.

Rojas, V., Guerrero, G. and Vargas, J. (2016) *Gendered trajectories through education, work and parenthood in Peru*, Working Paper 157, Oxford: Young Lives.

Rolleston, C. and James, Z. (2011) *The role of schooling in skill development: Evidence from Young Lives in Ethiopia, India, Peru and Vietnam*, Background Paper for UNESCO *Education for All Global Monitoring Report 2012*, Paris: UNESCO.

Rolleston, C. and Moore, R. (2018) *Young Lives school survey, 2016-17: Value-added analysis in India*, Department for International Development, 1 May (www.gov.uk/dfid-research-outputs/young-lives-school-survey-2016-17-value-added-analysis-in-india).

Rolleston, C., James, Z., Pasquier-Doumer, L. and Ngo Thi Minh Tam, T. (2013) *Making progress: Report of the Young Lives school survey in Vietnam*, Working Paper 100, Oxford: Young Lives.

Romero, M., Sandefur, J. and Sandholtz, W. (2017) *Can outsourcing improve Liberia's schools? Preliminary results from year one of a three-year randomized evaluation of partnership schools for Liberia*, Working Paper 462, Washington, DC: Center for Global Development.

Rossiter, J. (2016) *Scaling up access to quality early education in Ethiopia: Guidance from international experience*, Policy Paper 8, Oxford: Young Lives.

Rossiter, J., Woodhead, M., Rolleston, C. and Moore, R. (2018) *Delivering on a right to basic skills: Longitudinal view on the organization of school systems, educational opportunities and achievement*, Oxford: Oxford Department of International Development, University of Oxford.

Saeterdal, I., Lewin, S., Austvoll-Dahlgren, A., Glenton, C. and Munabi-Babigumira, S. (2014) 'Interventions aimed at communities to inform and/or educate about early childhood vaccination', *Cochrane Database of Systematic Reviews*, 11, CD010232. doi:10.1002/14651858. CD010232.pub2.

Salam, R., Faqqah, A., Sajjad, N., Lassi, Z.S., Das, J.K., Kaufman, M. and Bhutta, Z.A. (2016b) 'Improving adolescent sexual and reproductive health: A systematic review of potential interventions', *Journal of Adolescent Health*, 59(4), S11-S28.

Salam, R., Hooda, M., Das, J., Arshad, A., Lassi, Z., Middleton, P. and Bhutta, Z. (2016a) 'Interventions to improve adolescent nutrition: A systematic review and meta-analysis', *Journal of Adolescent Health*, 59(4), S29-S39.

Sameroff, A. (2009) *The transactional model of development: How children and contexts shape each other*, Washington, DC: American Psychological Association.

Sánchez, A. (2009) *Early nutrition and later cognitive achievement in developing countries. Background paper prepared for the Education for All Global Monitoring Report 2010*, Paris: UNESCO.

Sánchez, A. (2017) 'The structural relationship between early nutrition, cognitive skills and non-cognitive skills in four developing countries' (www.sciencedirect.com/science/article/pii/S1570677X17300849).

Sánchez, A. and Escobal, J. (forthcoming) *Survey attrition after 14 years of tracking children in four developing countries: The Young Lives study*, Working Paper: Oxford: Young Lives.

Serneels, P. and Dercon, S. (2014) *Aspirations, poverty and education: Evidence from India*, Working Paper 125, Oxford: Young Lives.

Sguassero, Y., de Onis, M., Bonotti, A.M. and Carroli, G. (2012) 'Community-based supplementary feeding for promoting the growth of children under five years of age in low and middle-income countries', *Cochrane Database of Systematic Reviews*, 6, CD005039, doi:10.1002/14651858.CD005039.pub3.

Shonkoff, J.P. (2010) 'Building a new biodevelopmental framework to guide the future of early childhood policy', *Child Development*, 81(1), 357-3.

Siegler, R.S., Duncan, G.J., Davis-Kean, P.E., Duckworth, K., Claessens, A., Engel, M., et al (2012) 'Early predictors of high school mathematics achievement', *Psychological Science*, 23(7), 691-7.

Singh, A. (2013) *Emergence and evolution of learning gaps across countries*, Working Paper 124, Oxford: Young Lives.

Singh, A. (2014) *Size and sources of the private school premium in test scores in India*, Working Paper 98, Oxford: Young Lives.

Singh, A. and Krutikova, S. (2017) *Starting together, growing apart: Gender gaps in learning from preschool to adulthood in four developing countries*, Working Paper 174, Oxford: Young Lives.

Singh, A., Park, A. and Dercon, S. (2013) 'School meals as a safety net: An evaluation of the Midday Meal Scheme in India', *Economic Development and Cultural Change*, 62(2), 275-306.

Singh, R. and Bangay, C. (2014) 'Low fee private schooling in India – More questions than answers? Observations from the Young Lives longitudinal research in Andhra Pradesh', *International Journal of Educational Development*, 39, 132-40.

Singh, R. and Mukherjee, P. (2017) *Comparison of the effects of government and private preschool education on the developmental outcomes of children: Evidence from Young Lives India*, Working Paper 167, Oxford: Young Lives.

Singh, R. and Vennam, U. (2016) *Factors shaping trajectories to child and early marriage: Evidence from Young Lives in India*, Working Paper 149, Oxford: Young Lives.

Singh, R., Galab, S., Reddy, P. Prudhvikar, P. and Benny, L. (2018) *Reaching the last child: Evidence from Young Lives India*, Country Report, Oxford: Young Lives.

Snilstveit, B., Stevenson, J., Phillips, D., Vojtkova, M., Gallagher, E., Schmidt, T., et al (2015) *Interventions for improving learning outcomes and access to education in low- and middle- income countries: A systematic review*, 3ie Systematic Review 24, London: International Initiative for Impact Evaluation (3ie).

Socialist Republic of Vietnam (2016) *The five year socio-economic development plan: 2016-2020*, Hanoi: Socialist Republic of Vietnam.

Stewart, F. (2000) 'Crisis prevention: Tackling horizontal inequalities', *Oxford Development Studies*, 28(3), 245-62.

Stewart, R., van Rooyen, C., Dickson, K., Majoro, M. and de Wet, T. (2010) *What is the impact of microfinance on poor people? A systematic review of evidence from sub-Saharan Africa*, London: EPPI-Centre, Social Science Research Unit, University of London.

Streuli, N. (2012) *Early childhood care and education in Peru: Evidence from Young Lives*, Policy Brief 18, Oxford: Young Lives.

Streuli, N., Vennam, U. and Woodhead, M. (2011) *Increasing choice or inequality? Pathways through early education in Andhra Pradesh, India*, Working Paper 58, Studies in Early Childhood Transitions, The Hague: Bernard van Leer Foundation.

Tafere, K. (2016) 'Inter-generational effects of early childhood shocks on human capital: Evidence from Ethiopia', Unpublished manuscript, Cornell University.

Tafere, Y. and Chuta, N. (2016) *Gendered trajectories of young people through school, work and marriage in Ethiopia*, Working Paper 155, Oxford: Young Lives.

Tafere, Y. and Pankhurst, A. (2015) *Can children in Ethiopian communities combine schooling with work?*, Working Paper 141, Oxford: Young Lives.

Thang, N. and Hang, N.T.T. (2018) *Leaving no one behind in a growing Vietnam: The story from Young Lives*, Country Report, Oxford: Young Lives.

Tredoux, C. and Dawes, A. (2018) *Latent growth modelling of mathematics and literacy skills at fifteen years in Ethiopia, India, Peru and Vietnam*, Working Paper 176, Oxford: Young Lives.

Tripney, J., Hombrados, J., Newman, M., Hovish, K., Brown, C., Steinka-Fry, K. and Wilkey, E. (2013) 'Technical and Vocational Education and Training (TVET) interventions to improve the employability and employment of young people in low- and middle-income countries: A systematic review', *Campbell Systematic Reviews*, doi:10.4073/csr.2013.9.

Tuan, T., Harpham, T. and Huong, N.T. (2004) 'Validity and reliability of the Self-reporting Questionnaire 20 items in Vietnam', *Hong Kong Journal of Psychiatry*, 14(3), 15-18.

UN (United Nations) (2000) *United Nations Millennium Declaration*, Resolution adopted by the General Assembly, 8th plenary meeting, 8 September, New York: UN.

UNDP (United Nations Development Programme) (2015) *Human Development Report 2015: Work for human development*, New York: UNDP.

UNESCO (United Nations Educational, Scientific and Cultural Organization) (2000) *The Dakar Framework for Action. Education for all: Meeting our collective commitments*, Paris: UNESCO.

UNESCO (2006) *Strong foundations. Early childhood care and education*, Paris: UNESCO

UNESCO (2013) *The global learning crisis*, Paris: UNESCO.

UNESCO (2015) *Education for all 2000-2015: Achievements and challenges*, EFA Global Monitoring Report 2015, Paris: UNESCO.

UNGA (United Nations General Assembly) (2015) *Transforming our world: The 2030 Agenda for Sustainable Development*, New York: UNGA.

UNGA (2017) *Work of the Statistical Commission pertaining to the 2030 Agenda for Sustainable Development*, New York: UNGA.

UN Habitat (2016) *Urbanization and development: Emerging futures, statistical annex,* Nairobi: United Nations Human Settlements Programme.

UNICEF (United Nations International Children's Emergency Fund) (2000) *Poverty reduction begins with children*, New York: UNICEF.

UNICEF (no date) *SDG Briefing Note 8: Early childhood development* (https://data.unicef.org/wp-content/uploads/2018/04/SDG-briefing-note-8_early-childhood-development.pdf).

UNICEF (2008) *The child care transition: A league table of early childhood education and care in economically advanced countries*, Innocenti Report Card 8, Florence: UNICEF Innocenti Research Centre.

UNICEF (2011) *The State of the World's Children 2011. Adolescence: An age of opportunity*, New York: UNICEF.

UNICEF (2015) *UNICEF's approach to scaling up nutrition for mothers and their children*, New York: UNICEF.

UNICEF (2017) *The State of the World's Children 2017. Children in a digital world*, New York: UNICEF.

UNICEF (2018) *Child marriage: Latest trends and future prospects*, New York: UNICEF.

UNICEF and The World Bank (2016) *Ending extreme poverty: A focus on children*, New York and Washington, DC: UNICEF and The World Bank.

UN Women (United Nations Entity for Gender Equality and the Empowerment of Women) (2015) *UN Women annual report 2014-15*, New York: UN Women.

van der Gaag, N., Pells, K. and Knowles, C. (2012) *Changing lives in a changing world: Young Lives children growing up*, Young Lives: Oxford.

Vandemoortele, M. (2018) *Inequality in attainment from early childhood to adolescence: Longitudinal evidence from Ethiopia*, Working Paper 177, Oxford: Young Lives.

Verstraeten, R., Roberfroid, D., Lachat, C., Leroy, J.L., Holdsworth, M., Maes, L. and Kolsteren, P.W. (2012) 'Effectiveness of preventive school-based obesity interventions in low- and middle-income countries: A systematic review', *American Journal of Clinical Nutrition*, 96(2), 415-38.

Vu, T.T.H. (2014) 'Ethnic minority children's and adults' perceptions and experiences of schooling in Vietnam: A case study of the Cham H'Roi', in M. Bourdillon and J. Boyden (eds) *Growing up in poverty: Findings from Young Lives* (pp 225-44), Basingstoke: Palgrave Macmillan.

Vythilingum, B., Field, S., Kafaar, Z., Baron, E., Stein, D.J., Sanders, L. and Honikman, S. (2013) 'Screening and pathways to maternal mental health care in a South African antenatal setting', *Archives of Women's Mental Health*, 16(5), 371-9.

Wachs, T. and Rahman, A. (2013) 'The nature and impact of risk and protective influences on children's development in low and middle-income countries', in P. Rebello-Britto, P. Engle and C. Super (eds) *Handbook of early childhood development research and its impact on global policy* (pp 85-122), Oxford: Oxford University Press.

Wachs, T., Black, M. and Engle, P. (2009) 'Maternal depression: A global threat to children's health, development, and behavior and to human rights', *Child Development Perspectives*, 3(1), 51-9.

Walker, S.P., Wachs, T.D., Grantham-McGregor, S., Black, M.M., Nelson, C.A., Huffman, S.L., et al (2011) 'Inequality in early childhood: Risk and protective factors for early child development', *The Lancet*, 378(9799), 1325-38.

Wamani, H., Åstrøm, A., Peterson, S., Tumwin, J. and Tylleskär, T. (2007) 'Boys are more stunted than girls in sub-Saharan Africa: A meta-analysis of 16 demographic and health surveys', *BMC Pediatrics*, 7, 17.

Wamoyi, J., Mshana, G., Mongi, A., Neke, N., Kapiga, S. and Changalucha, J. (2014) 'A review of interventions addressing structural drivers of adolescents' sexual and reproductive health vulnerability in sub-Saharan Africa: Implications for sexual health programming', *Reproductive Health*, 11, 88.

Watkins, K. and Quattri, M. (2016) *Child poverty, inequality and demography: Why sub-Saharan Africa matters for the Sustainable Development Goals*, London: Overseas Development Institute.

Watts, T.W., Duncan, G.J., Siegler, R.S. and Davis-Kean, P.E. (2014) 'What's past is prologue: Relations between early mathematics knowledge and high school achievement', *Educational Researcher*, 43(7), 352-60.

WFP (World Food Programme) (2013) *State of school feeding worldwide*, Rome: World Food Programme.

WHO (World Health Organization) (1994) *A user's guide to the Self Reporting Questionnaire SRQ20*, Geneva: WHO.

WHO (2014a) *Health for the world's adolescents: A second chance in the second decade*, Geneva: WHO.

WHO (2014b) *Global nutrition targets 2025: Stunting policy brief*, Geneva: WHO.

Woldehanna, T. (2011) 'The effects of early childhood education attendance on cognitive development: Evidence from urban Ethiopia', *Ethiopian Journal of Economics*, 20(1), 113-64.

Woldehanna, T., Berhman, J. and Araya, M. (2017) 'The effect of early childhood stunting on children's cognitive achievements: Evidence from young lives Ethiopia', *Ethiopian Journal of Health Development*, 31(2), 75-84.

Woldehanna, T., Gudisa, R., Tafere, Y. and Pankhurst, A. (2011) *Understanding changes in the lives of poor children: Initial findings from Ethiopia round 3 survey, Country report, Ethiopia*, Oxford: Young Lives.

Woodhead, M. (1996) *In search of the rainbow: Pathways to quality in large scale programmes for young disadvantaged children*, The Hague: Bernard Van Leer Foundation.

Woodhead, M. (2009) *Pathways through early childhood education in Ethiopia, India and Peru: Rights, equity and diversity*, Working Paper 54, Oxford: Young Lives.

Woodhead, M. (2016) *Early childhood development in the SDGs*, Policy Brief 28, Oxford: Young Lives.

Woodhead, M., Dornan, P. and Murray, H. (2013a) *What inequality means for children: Evidence from Young Lives*, Oxford: Young Lives.

Woodhead, M., Frost, M. and James, Z. (2013b) 'Does growth in private schooling contribute to Education for All? Evidence from a longitudinal, two cohort study in Andhra Pradesh, India', *International Journal of Educational Development*, 33(1), 65–73.

Woodhead, M., Rossiter, J., Dawes, A. and Pankhurst, A. (2017) *Scaling-up early learning in Ethiopia: Exploring the potential of O-Class*, Working Paper 163, Oxford: Young Lives.

Woodhead, M., Ames, P., Vennam, U., Abebe, W. and Streuli, N. (2009) *Equity and quality? Challenges for early childhood and primary education in Ethiopia, India and Peru*, Working Paper 55, The Hague: Bernard van Leer Foundation.

World Bank, The (2012) *World Development Report 2013: Jobs*, Washington, DC: The World Bank, doi:10.1596/978-0-8213-9575-2.

World Bank, The (2016a) *Poverty and shared prosperity 2016: Taking on inequality*, Washington, DC: The World Bank.

World Bank, The (2016b) *Ethiopia. Priorities for ending extreme poverty and promoting shared prosperity: Systematic country diagnostic*, Washington, DC: The World Bank.

World Bank, The (2017) *Peru. Systematic country diagnostic*, Washington, DC: The World Bank.

World Bank, The (2018a) *India. Realizing the promise of prosperity: Systematic country diagnostic*, Washington, DC: The World Bank.

World Bank, The (2018b) *World Development Report 2018: Learning to realize education's promise*, Washington, DC: The World Bank.

YMAPS (Young Marriage and Parenthood Study) (2018) *Understanding child marriage: Insights from comparative research*, Policy Brief 1, Oxford: Young Lives.

Young Lives (2012) *The future we want: Learning from children's experiences of sustainable development*, London: Save the Children UK.

Young Lives (2015a) *How gender shapes adolescence: Diverging paths and opportunities*, Policy Brief 22, Oxford: Young Lives.

Young Lives (2015b) *Young Lives theory of change*, Oxford: Young Lives.

Young Lives (2016) *Towards a better future? Hopes and fears from Young Lives* (www.younglives.org.uk/content/young-lives-theory-change).

Zharkevich, I., Roest, J. and Vu, T.T.H. (2016) *Gendered trajectories through school, work and marriage in Vietnam*, Working Paper 158, Oxford: Young Lives.

Zolkoski, S.M. and Bullock, L.M. (2012) 'Resilience in children and youth: A review', *Children and Youth Services Review*, 34(12), 2295–303.

Appendix 1: How Young Lives measures cognitive skills

The term 'cognitive skill' is widely used in Young Lives research. The instruments, or tests, described below are drawn and adapted from other studies and used to measure domains of ability that are related to cognitive skills. Where the same ability was measured at different ages, tests were modified across the rounds to ensure that they would be age-appropriate. Since the tests are translated between and within countries, ensuring their linguistic equivalence is a major challenge and so significant psychometric assessment has been undertaken (see Cueto and Leon, 2012).

Receptive vocabulary. The test measures hearing vocabulary, providing an indicator of vocabulary acquisition (the assessor says a word and asks the child to point to a picture that depicts the stimulus word). Performance is strongly related to reading comprehension. In the Older Cohort, the Peabody Picture Vocabulary Test (PPVT) was administered at all rounds. In the Younger Cohort, it was administered when the children were 5 and 8 years old (Rounds 2 and 3). For this cohort and following psychometric analysis, the test was adapted for rounds 4 and 5. The test was shortened and the word order adjusted to take account of item difficulty in the various languages (see Cueto and Leon, 2012). These later shortened tests are not strictly equivalent to the original PPVT, though they are conceptually the same and use the same target pictures and words for retained items. Main languages of adaptation for which psychometric analysis has been undertaken are Telugu (India), Vietnamese, and Oromifa, Tigrinya and Amharic (Ethiopia). In Peru in all rounds for both cohorts, the Spanish version (PPVT-R) was used for Castellano speakers and translated for Quechua children.

Reading comprehension. At 8 years of age, children were assessed on reading comprehension using the Early Grade Reading Assessment (EGRA). This oral assessment test measures basic building blocks of reading acquisition, including emergent literacy, understanding sentences, and listening with comprehension. EGRA has been used widely in many low- and middle-income countries by RTI International (Gove and Wetterberg, 2011). In places, the tests were adapted (see Cueto and Leon, 2012). At age 15 years, children were assessed on a reading comprehension test that measured literacy at basic, intermediate and advanced levels including using items drawn from the Organisation for Economic Co-operation and Development's Programme for International Student Assessment (PISA) and the UNESCO Literacy Assessment and Monitoring Programme (Tredoux and Dawes, 2018).

Cognitive Developmental Assessment (CDA). The CDA was developed by the International Association for the Evaluation of Educational Achievement. Only the quantity subtest of the CDA (CDA-Q) is used in the study to assess children at 5 years of age (Cueto et al, 2009).

Mathematics achievement. Young Lives mathematics tests used in the household surveys from 5 years of age contain items of increasing difficulty drawn from the PISA (Programme for International Student Assessment) and TIMMS (Trends in International Mathematics and Science Study). They are answered in the child's preferred language. These items have been used to compare across the country samples and in some analyses a number of common mathematics items are used to compare growth in abilities over time. However, ceiling effects on the common item set become apparent by age 12, requiring the use of alternative approaches for comparisons of the same child across time (Tredoux and Dawes, 2018).

Appendix 2: Growth recovery – is it real or an artefact of measurement?

Whether children can recover early losses in growth and development is a complex question and is subject to debate. Insofar as physical recovery after infancy may be possible and also be associated with other developmental benefits, not to support recovery wastes later opportunities; on the other hand, if children cannot recover, a focus on later ages could deflect attention from the critical early years.

Is physical recovery real? Most Young Lives studies use height-for-age Z scores (HAZ) to track change. This approach first defines stunting as when the child is more than two standard deviations below the median height of a reference population of children of the same gender and age (using WHO norms). Change in HAZ is then used to identify recovery and faltering. Leroy and colleagues (2015) make the case for an alternative measure, height-for-age differences (HAD), arguing that while HAZ shows early post-infancy recovery (termed by some people as 'catch-up growth'), HAD does not. The authors therefore argue that any indication of recovery is simply a function of the measure. HAD measures absolute change (so, for example, a five-centimetre difference from expected height is thought to be equally important for babies and five-year-olds). HAZ accounts for the growing height dispersion at older age (so a five-centimetre difference for babies is thought worse than for five-year-olds). A constant absolute difference of five centimetres from the expected height under HAD would show as no change between infancy and 5 years, but under HAZ it would suggest a level of recovery.

This debate is ongoing. An important reason for thinking something significant is happening when children's growth status improves (according to HAZ measures) after early childhood is that when children recover physically, this recovery has itself been linked to better cognitive outcomes, independent of early circumstances. If meaningful recovery did not happen, or were not linked to these outcome improvements, we would not expect to see such a relationship.

Is Young Lives equipped to track physical recovery? Young Lives is a general purpose observational study. It is not a specific study of nutrition, nor a causal experiment following interventions. The study collects relevant data both on child height and on a wide set of potential determinants of physical growth. The four-country basis, coupled with the size and diversity of the sample, gives Young Lives a powerful call to global relevance. However, the study does not have the frequent data points in utero or infancy needed to contribute to debates about the factors *within* the first 1,000 days of life.

Can children recover all their early losses? The phrase 'recovery' is used as it is not clear that all early losses can be 'caught up', and in some cases, for example child mortality caused by under-nutrition, this cannot be the case. When children's cognitive test results are considered, even though children who recover perform better than those who do not recover, those who have never been stunted do the best of all. These findings suggest greater attention to growth and nutrition in middle childhood and adolescence, not less attention to early life.

What is the importance for policy and programming? Prevention is better than cure, which necessitates a focus on the earliest point in life. There is no 'choice' between early or later investments. Evidence of recovery and faltering does suggest there may be returns from programming at older ages also (such as service improvements, social protection and feeding programmes). Less is known, particularly in adolescence, about whether physical recovery can be affected by policy and there is a case to investigate whether this is possible through experimental trials.

Appendix 3: Variables used in analyses of predictors of the development of language and mathematics abilities from 5 to 15 years

PREDICTOR VARIABLES

All countries
Household wealth (rounds 1 and 2 averaged): Young Lives Wealth Index (Briones, 2017). The index comprises consumer durables, access to services and housing quality on a continuous scale of wealth. Higher values reflect higher household wealth.

All countries
Maternal education (round 1): total years of education (school and post-school).

All countries
Hours of school and study (rounds 3, 4 and 5): total hours per day the child reports as being spent at school plus time (in hours) reported as studying after the school per day (averaged over rounds 3, 4 and 5 per child).

Hours of chores and tasks (rounds 3, 4 and 5): total hours per day the child reports as being spent on caring for others in the household, and doing household chores (such as cleaning and fetching water) and household tasks (such as assisting on the family plot). Total hours for all three are averaged over rounds 3, 4 and 5 per child.

All countries
Preschool participation (round 2: for all countries except Ethiopia [in round 3]): country-specific scaling by preschool provision type was used with higher scores awarded to what is likely to be better provision based on other Young Lives study findings.

Peru: no preschool = 0; public PRONOEI = 01; Public Centro Educativo Inicial (CEI) Público (Public Jardine) = 02; private centre-based CEI = 03.

Ethiopia: no preschool = 0; public/community-based = 01; private = 02.

Vietnam: no preschool = 0; public/community-based = 01; private = 02.

United Andhra Pradesh (India): no preschool = 0; public/community-based = 01; private = 02.

All countries
Maternal mental health (round 1): Self Reporting Questionnaire (SRQ20) (WHO, 1994). A high score indicates risk of common mental disorder (anxiety and depression). In the model the scale was reversed for ease of interpretation. The SRQ20 has established reliability and validity at acceptable levels in many developing countries, including Vietnam, India, Peru and Ethiopia (Harpham et al, 2003, 2005; Tuan et al, 2004; Bennett et al, 2016).

All countries
Growth stunting (round 1 at age 1 and round 2 at 5 years): each child is given a score based on their growth status[1] at each age, as follows: normal height-for-age = 0; stunted = 1; severely stunted = 2. Scores at age 1 year and age 5 years were aggregated, thus the early growth stunting score had a range of 0-4.

All countries
Early quantitative skills (round 3): Cognitive Development Assessment (CDA) quantity concepts (15 items). For psychometry, see Cueto et al (2009).

CHRONOLOGICALLY LATEST OUTCOME VARIABLE

All countries
Reading comprehension (round 5): reading comprehension test raw score at 15 years. The test has five sets of items that assess basic to advanced literacy. Items are drawn from publicly available international tests (PIRLS) (Young Lives internal documentation). The number of

items varies by country. Psychometric properties were established using both classical test theory and item response theory (IRT) for round 4. Round 5 tests were based on piloted items in each country to establish random responses (guessing), item difficulty and item discrimination. Items with sound properties were selected. Psychometry on round 5 had not been completed at the time of this analysis.

LATENT GROWTH VARIABLES

Latent growth in receptive vocabulary
Measured at ages 5 (round 2), 8 (round 3), 12 (round 4) and 15 years (round 5) using the child's total score in the same language at each of these age points. Minor languages were excluded as samples were too small for analysis.

Peru: Peabody Picture Vocabulary Test (PPVT-R) in Spanish.

India, Vietnam and Ethiopia: receptive vocabulary was measured using translated versions of PPVT-III that were adapted to ensure correct order of item difficulty (and shortened) following IRT analyses in round 3.

At the time of this analysis, psychometric analyses and Rasch scores were not available for round 5. For earlier rounds, see Cueto et al (2009); Cueto and Leon (2012); Leon and Singh (2017). Due to adaptation, the test is not strictly equivalent to the PPVT.

Raw score totals were used in analyses. Languages used in the models were as follows:

India: Telugu.

Vietnam: Vietnamese.

Ethiopia: Oromifa, Tigrinya and Amharic. Tests in each of the three languages had the same number of items, and items in each language were ordered in terms of difficulty. Scores were combined in one sample rather than modelling each language separately.

Latent growth in mathematics ability
Mathematics ability was measured at 8 (round 3), 12 (round 4) and 15 years (round 5). Tests increase in difficulty at each age point. As

the tests were not equivalent across time points, total scores at each point were transformed to standard normal deviates (Z scores) for comparative purposes. For Young Lives psychometric analyses, see Cueto et al (2009); Cueto and Leon (2012). Psychometry for rounds 4 and 5 was not available as the time of this study.

Note

[1] Stunting: HAZ > 2 standard deviations below the population median; severe stunting: HAZ > 3 standard deviations below the population median.

The latent growth curve in each case was constituted by a latent variable representing the intercept, and a latent variable representing slope/change. Both were modelled as varying randomly across individual children.

Because we attempt to equate the variables and compare their relative importance, we report only standardised coefficients, and hence these are not interpretable in terms of the unscaled variables described in this table.

Child age was controlled in both models by entering it as an exogenous variable with a directional effect on the latent variable representing the intercept component of the latent growth curve. We do not show child age in any of the model diagrams, as it is a control rather than substantive element.

Additional variables of emotional wellbeing, substance misuse and antisocial behaviour, used in the Peru models, are not described here. For details, see Tredoux and Dawes (2018).

Index